FELT TOYS

for little ones

Handmade Playsets to Spark Imaginative Play

Jessica Peck
of Sweetie Pie Bakery

stashBOOKS®

an imprint of C&T Publishing

Text copyright © 2013 by Jessica Peck

Photography and Artwork copyright © 2013 by C&T Publishing, Inc.

PUBLISHER: Amy Marson

CREATIVE DIRECTOR: Gailen Runge

ART DIRECTOR: Kristy Zacharias

EDITORS: Lynn Koolish and Deb Rowden

TECHNICAL EDITORS: Ann Haley, Teresa Stroin, Sandy Peterson, Mary Flynn, and Nanette Zeller

COVER/BOOK DESIGNER: April Mostek

PRODUCTION COORDINATOR: Jenny Davis

PRODUCTION EDITOR: Joanna Burgarino

ILLUSTRATOR: Lon Eric Craven

PHOTO ASSISTANT: Mary Peyton Peppo

PHOTOGRAPHY BY Diane Pedersen and Nissa Brehmer of C&T Publishing, Inc., unless otherwise noted

Published by Stash Books, an imprint of C&T Publishing, Inc., P.O. Box 1456, Lafayette, CA 94549

Library of Congress Cataloging-in-Publication Data

Peck, Jessica, 1982-

  Felt toys for little ones : handmade playsets to spark imaginative play / Jessica Peck.

    pages cm

  ISBN 978-1-60705-767-3 (soft cover)

1. Soft toy making. 2. Felt work. 3. Sewing. 4. Handicraft. I. Title.

  TT174.3.P44 2013

  745.592'4--dc23

                      2013013789

Printed in China

10 9 8 7 6 5 4 3 2 1

Dedication

This book is dedicated to my three favorite redheads, who have allowed me to reach my dreams through all of their love, support and inspiration: an abundance of love and gratitude to Jason, Ephraim, and Aeris.

Acknowledgments

I am so honored to have had such a wonderful support system in creating this book.

Without the patience and encouragement of my team at C&T Publishing, this book would not have been possible. Thank you for guiding me through this process and being so understanding with my thousands of questions.

Much generosity has been shown to help in the production of all of the projects in this book. Aurifil, Dear Stella, Michael Miller Fabrics, P&B Textiles, PCP Group (Pellon/Legacy), and Prym-Dritz Corporation are gracious companies that have all lent their support. Special thanks to Wacom Technology Corporation for aiding in the production of technical illustrations. Most importantly, National Nonwovens wool felts have been my premier choice over the years. I have been working with Christin and the dedicated team at National Nonwovens for years and cannot thank them enough for supplying all of the felt for this book.

Thank you to my beautiful babies, Ephraim and Aeris. My children are my main source of inspiration. They aid me in each project, every step of the way, from inspiration to production.

And to my incredibly supportive husband, thank you for your patience. It is with your love and belief in me that my dreams are made possible.

Contents

Introduction

There is not a moment from my childhood that I cannot remember being enveloped with a mother's touch. From the Care Bears and rainbows that hung on my bedroom wall to a sunny yellow gingham quilt, from fields of lavender flowers draped over my canopy bed to a velvet outfit to match my favorite Cabbage Patch doll, the special touches were all there. Mothers and grandmothers took time from their own lives to create something special for mine. Even as a small child I understood the significance of the handmade items in my life, and as soon as I had children of my own, I knew I wanted them to have the same.

As I began creating things for my two children—clothes and blankets, duvets and throw pillows—I soon learned that I didn't want just beautiful curtains to hang on bedroom walls but things we could enjoy together, things we could use together. When I thought back to those items from my childhood, the most joy I had came from when my father would lift down the Care Bears and let me float off on a bed of clouds to Care-a-lot. This world of imagination and wonder is what was missing in those beautiful pieces I was creating for our home. My children and I could not interact with one another through a custom-covered lampshade.

I began taking notes on the playroom floor. As my children played I watched what they played with and how they played with it. I created designs and then gave them to my children and watched how they responded, what pieces they pulled off, and what pieces fell off. More often than anything, they brought the toy back to me. They were offering me entry into their world of imagination, where we could play tea party or sell football tickets. Re-creating a world where they could go grocery shopping and choose produce, pay the cashier, and bag their own groceries allowed them opportunities for role play and creativity.

The greatest joy from creating toys and play spaces for my children was introducing imaginative play through my handmade items. The benefits of imaginative play in young children are innumerable, especially when playing with loved ones.

Photos by Jessica Peck

Getting Started

Before you begin any project, it is important to understand your materials and their applications. The types of materials you choose have a great impact on the longevity and wear of a product. There is nothing worse than finishing a project only to find out you didn't use the proper materials.

Sewing Tools

Cutting and Measuring

Even a novice sewist would tell you that never, under any circumstances whatsoever, should the fabric scissors cut anything other than fabric! Sewists are very partial to their scissors, which may be why they have collections of them.

I mention four types of scissors throughout this book. Although it is not essential to have them all, it is helpful, as each pair discussed has its own specific use.

DRESSMAKING SHEARS

The first pair of scissors a sewist should invest in is a great pair of shears. While shears are offered in a wide range of prices, the most important thing to keep in mind is that these scissors should be used solely for fabric. This practice will ensure the longevity of even an economical pair. For use on felt, I have a secondary pair of dressmaking shears marked with a ribbon so I do not confuse the two.

EMBROIDERY SCISSORS

Embroidery scissors are a great addition to any sewing kit and usually the second pair that one would add after a great pair of fabric shears. They usually measure about 4″ in length, making them ideal for doing detailed work and taking on the go.

CRAFT SCISSORS

Craft scissors are an economical choice to extend the life of the rest of your scissors; use them on interfacing as well as paper and templates.

BLUNT-TIP SCISSORS

Although not used too often, when they are called for, blunt-tip scissors are extremely helpful. For example, when you are clipping around the curve of a seam, blunt-tip scissors are an ideal choice so that you do not accidentally cut the sewn section. Blunt-tip scissors are also useful for cutting many lightweight and sheer fabrics. The soft end will prevent fabric from fraying when cut.

ROTARY CUTTER

A rotary cutter, offering accuracy and precision, is often a quilter's favored choice for cutting fabric. While most of the projects in this book do not call for long cuts of fabric, some do use the rotary cutter's replacement blades. Swapping the straight blade for a scalloped or pinking blade lets you create beautiful decorative edges. I recommend Olfa's Deluxe Ergonomic Rotary Cutter. Not only is the handle comfortable, but the blades are easily interchangeable, which is helpful when working on these felt projects.

CUTTING MAT AND CLEAR RULER

For use with a rotary cutter, a cutting mat and clear ruler are essential. I recommend Olfa's 24″ × 36″ Self-Healing Rotary Mat along with a 6″ × 24″ Non-Slip, Frosted Advantage Acrylic Ruler. It is helpful to have a ruler as long as your mat is wide so you can benefit from the full capacity of your cutting mat.

sewing tools

Pins and Needles

There are several different types of sewing pins that vary by head, point, and length.

For the projects in this book, I recommend pins with plastic, ball-shaped heads and sharp points. These are great for felt or fabric projects and come in long and short lengths. I like pinning the felt projects together and removing the pins as I hand sew. I recommend Dritz Ball Point Pins, both long and short. Keep in mind that some plastic heads will melt under the heat of an iron, so be careful when you take projects to the ironing board.

The projects in this book use two types of needles: sewing machine needles and hand embroidery needles. Check with the manual for the particular sizes needed for your sewing machine; fabrics in this book require a sharp or universal needle and a medium/heavy-weight needle. For hand embroidery, I recommend Dritz Embroidery needles. These needles have a larger eye than other needles and will accommodate several strands of embroidery floss. Change needles often, since wool felt will dull them quickly.

Marking Tools

I have learned that marking tools are a very personal preference. What works best for me are Clover Pen-Style Chaco Liners. Although the chalk does create some dust in a sewing machine, these liners make the most precise marks on fabrics and are easiest to remove. Pilot FriXion Erasable Gel Pens are another great choice for marking on fabric. They make really precise marks that will disappear with the heat of an iron. They do tend to leave a waxy residue, but it can easily be scraped off.

Template Paper

One of my favorite tools is tracing paper. It comes on a roll 12″ or 24″ wide. I have found it to be perfect for tracing sewing patterns. The 12″ roll is sufficient for most of the projects in this book.

Materials

Felt

There are several different types of felt, but three are best for my crafting purposes: bamboo felt, craft felt, and wool felt.

BAMBOO FELT

Rather new to the market, bamboo offers a sustainable option by combining 50% bamboo fibers and 50% rayon fibers. The result is extremely soft yet incredibly durable, making it a premier choice for soft toys and children's products.

CRAFT FELT

Craft felt, also known as artificial felt, is a blend of wool and a significant amount of acrylic fibers. Craft felts are a great material for working with children on art projects or for pieces that will not get much handling. However, craft felts would not be the best choice for a toy because the high count of acrylic fibers will result in more pilling than you get from other felts. A better choice for a toy or an object that will endure a good amount of handling would be a wool blend, with at least 35% wool fibers.

WOOL FELT

Wool felt is composed of 100% wool, with no artificial fibers. While wool felt offers a terrific hand to a finished project, it can be more expensive and it is not necessary to ensure the longevity of an item.

I recommend using wool blends or bamboo felt for the projects in this book. National Nonwovens offers products with a hand that I love as well as a wide array of color choices.

Fabric

Several types of fabrics are mentioned in this book: cotton, duck cloth, and vinyl. The most important thing to note when using woven fabric is the grain line. The grain line is composed of threads moving in opposite directions. When you look closely, you will notice the structure of the fabric, called the *warp* and the *weft*.

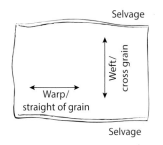

When you place your templates onto the fabric, pay attention to the orientation. Place the arrow on the template in line with the grain. Placing the template at an angle to the grain could cause the cut piece to stretch and fray, compromising the end result.

COTTON FABRICS

Always prewash cotton fabrics before use. If there is any shrinkage, it is best for that to happen before you create a project. This is especially important if you are using several different types of cotton, since the amount of shrinkage will vary from fabric to fabric. It is also important to note the direction of the print on the fabric that you have chosen. Some prints are directional, meaning that if you look at them from a different angle they appear upside down or sideways. You may need additional yardage for a directional print.

DUCK CLOTH

Duck cloth is a very specific type of cotton fabric. It is woven with two yarns in the warp and one yarn in the weft, creating a tight, heavy weave. Different weights of cotton duck are indicated by numbers: Larger numbers denote lighter fabrics and smaller numbers denote heavier fabrics.

VINYL

Vinyl and coated fabrics present sewing challenges. When working with vinyl, it is important not to fold the fabric. Roll the fabric for storage to prevent it from creasing. When sewing with vinyl, consider using a Teflon presser foot or placing tissue paper over the fabric. Tissue will allow you to sew smoothly while still seeing the vinyl underneath.

Thread

The type of thread you choose for a sewing project will affect the integrity of the end project as well as the condition of your sewing machine. For the projects in this book, I recommend Aurifil 50/2 (50-weight, 2-ply) cotton threads. They are strong but lightweight and keep your machine very clean, while some other threads tend to fray and leave a lot of lint behind. For embroidery, I recommend 6-strand cotton floss, such as DMC embroidery floss. It comes in any color I need and is very easy to work with.

Stuffing

Two of the most popular options for stuffing felt toys are cotton stuffing and fiberfill. Fiberfill is created from polyester, making it a more economical choice. Fiberfill is also nonallergenic and therefore a great option for those with allergy considerations. Cotton stuffing offers a natural alternative to fiberfill. When using either product, be sure to pull apart the fibers and gently fluff the stuffing before placing it into the toy. I find that this method prevents lumps and allows the toy to take shape better.

Foam

Some of the projects are filled with a ½″, 1″, or 4″ layer of foam. For foam 1″ or thinner, I cut the pieces to the desired size with scissors. If the foam is greater than 1″ thick, I use an electric knife.

stuffing

A Few Key Terms

Blind stitch: A sewing stitch visible on only one side of the fabric.

Right side: The side of the fabric that you want to show, the side *without* the pattern construction markings.

Wrong side: The side you do not want to show, the side *with* the pattern construction markings.

If you notice that the two sides of a piece of felt feel different, use the softer side as the right *side, and the rougher side as the* wrong *side.*

General Sewing Notes

As with any specialized craft, there are several rules and methods involved in making felt toys. The following are some guidelines to supply you with a basic knowledge of sewing that will be helpful when creating the projects in this book.

All seams in these projects are ¼˝ unless stated otherwise. To obtain a ¼˝ seam, you can often align the edge of your sewing machine's presser foot with the side of the fabric. Measure to check the width of your presser foot. There are feet made especially for sewing ¼˝ seams, and some even have a guide on the side to prevent you from driving off course. If you're a beginning sewist, one of these would be an investment worth making.

When machine sewing, remember to lockstitch at the beginning and end of each line of stitching. Newer machines have a button to press that will make a knot. With older models, backstitch a few stitches and then go forward again to secure the stitches. This rule does not apply if you are basting or if you will need to pull the threads for gathering, which a knot or backstitch will prevent you from doing.

When sewing with embroidery floss, you will usually separate the six strands. For most of the stitches in this book, you need only two strands of embroidery floss. For some of the detail running stitches, where you want a thicker line for decorative purposes, use all six strands. You will quickly get a feel for what you're comfortable with sewing and can use your own discretion.

Foamcore board is used to support quite a few projects in this book. Foamcore board is paper mounted on a foam core. It is generally found in sheets ³⁄₁₆˝ thick, 20˝ × 30˝, at office supply stores, craft stores, and art stores. To cut foamcore board, use a craft knife with a very sharp blade. I recommend using a cork-backed metal ruler to prevent slipping while you are making straight cuts. If you are cutting curves, go slowly and take a few passes until the knife cuts through all the layers of paper and foam.

In some situations, adhesives are called for to attach the foamcore board supports. I recommend using basic school glue, unless otherwise stated. It is nontoxic and holds remarkably well. Use a very small amount of glue, just enough to tack the felt to the board. I find that other adhesives, such as hot glue, dry too quickly and too thick, creating a bumpy finish on the other side of the felt.

For circle patterns, dimensions are given for the diameter, or width, of the circle. Use the circle patterns provided on the CD or a circle template or compass to complete the projects in this book. Circle templates and compasses come in different sizes and can be found at your local art supply store.

The patterns for most of the shapes used for the projects in this book are found on the attached CD, and they print out on 8½˝ × 11˝ sheets. Directions to draw and cut a few of the larger shapes without patterns are included in the project cutting charts.

caution: *Small children may choke on beads, buttons, snaps, and other small pieces if they come loose.*

Tea Party Treats

One of my favorite movies is *The Little Princess* with Shirley Temple. It's the story of a little girl who is forced to live as a maid in a boarding school because her father is believed to have died in a war. My favorite scene is when Sara wakes up to discover a room of luxury. Her tattered clothes have been replaced with fine satins and velvets, her empty hearth has been replaced with a warm fire, and her hungry belly is waiting to be filled with sausages, warm tea, and treats. This moment seemed so magical to me as a child, and every time I have a tea party with my daughter, I go back there. Tea parties are a way to transport any child to a moment of fantasy.

Lemon

Part of having a tea party is all the dainty details. Lemon and sugar are standard enhancements to any good cup of tea.

MATERIALS • Makes one lemon.

Patterns can be found on page CD1.

Material	Amount	Cut
Yellow felt	3″ × 6″	Cut 8 lemon segments (A) and 1 lemon rind (C).
White felt	3″ × 3″	Cut 1 lemon pith (D).
Ivory felt	3″ × 3″	Cut 1 lemon segment base (B).
Embroidery floss—yellow, ivory, white		

Lemon Assembly

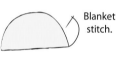

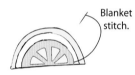

1. Using a running stitch, stitch the lemon segments (A) to the lemon segment base (B).

2. Fold the lemon rind (C) in half, wrong sides together. Blanket stitch around the perimeter of the open edge to join the layers.

3. Fold the pith (D) over the folded edge of the rind (C) and stitch around the curved edge of the pith, using a running stitch, to attach the layers.

4. Fold the lemon segment base (B) with attached segments over the pith (D), and stitch the curved edge of the base (B) with a blanket stitch to complete the lemon.

Sugar Cube

MATERIALS • Makes three sugar cubes.

Patterns can be found on page CD1.

Material	Amount	Cut
White felt	3″ × 6″	Cut 3 sugar cubes (A).
Iridescent glass beads (*optional*)		
Embroidery floss—white		
Stuffing		

Sugar Cube Assembly

Blanket stitch.

1. Referring to the diagram, fold up the bottom of the sugar cube (A) and stitch each side in turn with a blanket stitch.

2. Fold up the top of the sugar cube (A) and stitch the next 2 corners with a blanket stitch.

Blanket stitch.

3. Fold the last edge over the top of the sugar cube (A) and blanket stitch around the top perimeter. Leave a small opening to stuff the sugar cube (A) before closing it.

4. Repeat Steps 1–3 to create 2 more sugar cubes.

Blind stitch.

5. Create a base from 2 sugar cubes and place the third on top. Using a needle and thread, secure the sugar cubes together. If you have chosen to embellish the sugar cubes, now you can sew on the glass beads to complete them. (*A note about beads:* Be sure to use your judgment regarding the safety of adding such embellishments. If they are for a small child, you may choose to embellish the sugar cubes with embroidered French knots instead.)

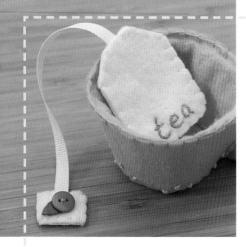

Tea Bag

MATERIALS • Makes two tea bags.

Patterns can be found on page CD2.

Material	Amount	Cut
White felt	7″ × 9″	Cut 4 rectangles ¾″ × 1″ for tea bag tag (A) and 4 tea bags (B).
Green felt	2″ × 2″	Cut 2 tea leaves (C).
Grosgrain ribbon, ¼″ wide—white	8″	Cut 2 pieces, 4″ long.
¼″ buttons—purple, orange	1 each	
Embroidery floss—white, purple, orange		

Tea Bag Assembly

1. Using a needle and thread, secure a green leaf (C) to a tag (A).

2. Using a needle and embroidery floss, sew the button onto the tag, covering the bottom of the leaf. Set aside.

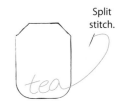

Split stitch.

3. Use a split stitch to embroider the word *tea* to a tea bag (B).

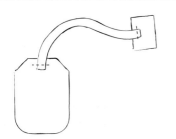

4. On the wrong side of another tea bag (B), position the ribbon at the top and sew it down by machine. Sew the other end of the ribbon, by machine, on the wrong side of a tag (A) without the embellishments.

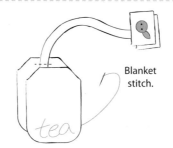

Blanket stitch.

5. Place the embellished tea bag (B) over the tea bag (B) with the attached ribbon. Stitch around the perimeter with a blanket stitch. Repeat with tag (A).

6. Repeat Steps 1–5 to create another tea bag.

Tray

No tea party is complete without a tray. I designed this tray with handles so a tea party can travel from a teddy bear picnic to a homemade fort. Everything should be able to be on the go.

MATERIALS • Makes one tray.

Patterns can be found on pages CD3–CD8.

Material	Amount	Cut
White felt, 36″ wide	⅔ yard	Cut 2 tray bases (A), 4 tray handles (B), 4 tray sides (C), and 4 tray ends (D).
Foamcore board	8″ × 12″	Cut 1 tray base support (A1).
fast2fuse heavy double-sided stiff fusible interfacing	6″ × 13″	Cut 2 tray side supports (C1) and 2 tray end supports (D1).
Embroidery floss—white		
Stuffing		

Tray Assembly

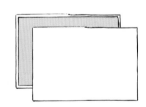

1. Place 2 tray handles (B) right sides together. Sew along the upper and lower curve of each handle by machine, leaving the ends open.

2. Turn the handle (B) right side out and stuff. Repeat Steps 1 and 2 to create the second handle. Set aside.

3. Glue the foamcore board tray base support (A1) centered between the 2 tray bases (A), with right sides facing out.

4. Following the manufacturer's directions, fuse the wrong side of the felt to both sides of the interfacing for each tray side (C). Make 2. Fuse the wrong side of the felt to 1 side of the interfacing for each tray end (D).

5. Slip a handle between the remaining piece of felt and the interfaced side of a tray end (D) and fuse. Repeat for the other tray end. Reinforce the handle attachments by machine.

6. Use a blanket stitch to attach the bottom edge of a tray end (D) to the tray base (A).

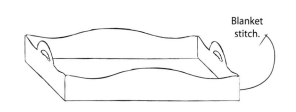

Blanket stitch.

7. When you reach the corner, continue to stitch along the base, adding a tray side (C), and so on, until both ends and both sides have been attached.

8. Once you have all of the sides attached, blanket stitch up each corner in turn.

9. To complete the tray, use a blanket stitch to sew around the top perimeter.

Petit Fours

This basic petit four pattern has endless variations. You could add embellishments such as trim or rickrack, buttons, or fabric flowers, or just let your little one decorate the cut-out felt with fabric markers before it gets sewn together.

MATERIALS • Makes three petit fours.

Patterns can be found on page CD9.

Material	Amount	Cut
Pink felt	9″ × 12″	Cut 1 petit four base (A) and 1 petit four bottom (B).
Yellow felt	9″ × 12″	Cut 1 petit four base (A) and 1 petit four bottom (B).
Aqua felt	9″ × 12″	Cut 1 petit four base (A) and 1 petit four bottom (B).
White felt	3″ × 3″	Cut 3 petit four embellishments (C).
2″-thick foam	3″ × 8″	Cut 3 cubes 2″ × 2″ × 2″.
Embroidery floss—pink, yellow, aqua, white		

Petit Four Assembly

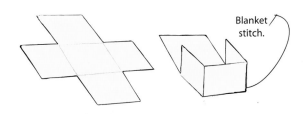

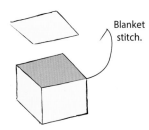

1. Fold the ends of the petit four base (A) up with right sides facing out. Blanket stitch the edges together, an edge at a time.

2. Insert the foam into the petit four base (A). Position the petit four bottom (B) over the opening in the petit four base (A) and the added foam. Beginning in a corner, blanket stitch around the perimeter.

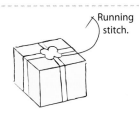

3. Sew an embellishment to the top of the treat.

4. Repeat Steps 1–3 to complete the other 2 petit four treats.

Teapot and Teacups

All little children enjoy tea parties, little boys too! I created this teapot with modern details to appeal to whatever your child may be into. By adding your own embellishments, you can make the teapot look dramatically different.

MATERIALS • Makes one teapot and two cups.

Patterns can be found on pages CD10–CD12.

Material	Amount	Cut
White felt, 36″ wide	¾ yard	Cut 6 teapot sides (A), 2 teapot lids (C), 1 teapot lid side (D), 2 teapot bases (E), 4 teacup sides (I), 4 teacup bases (J), and 4 (2 and 2 reversed) teacup handles (K).
Red felt	2 sheets 9″ × 12″	Cut 2 (1 and 1 reverse) teapot spouts (F), 1 spout end (G), and 2 (1 and 1 reversed) teapot handles (H).
Colored scraps for polka dots and teacup stripes	10 squares 4″ × 4″	Cut 10 teapot polka dots (B) and 14 rectangles ¼″ × 2″ for teacup stripes.
Foamcore board	4″ × 4″ square	Cut 1 teapot base support (E1).
½″-thick foam	5″ × 5″ square	Cut 1 teapot lid (C).
Heavyweight fusible interfacing	6″ × 9″ rectangle	Cut 2 teacup side supports (I1) and 2 teacup base supports (J1).
Felt ball	1″ diameter	
Embroidery floss—white; thread to correspond with polka dot felt		
Stuffing		

Teapot Assembly

1. Place 2 teapot sides (A) right sides together. By machine, sew from dot to dot along a long side.

2. Add another teapot side (A) in the same manner. Repeat until all 6 sides are joined.

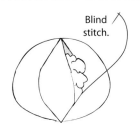

Blind stitch.

3. When you sew the final seam, be sure to leave a 2″ opening in the side to turn the teapot right side out. Stuff the teapot and sew the opening shut using a blind stitch.

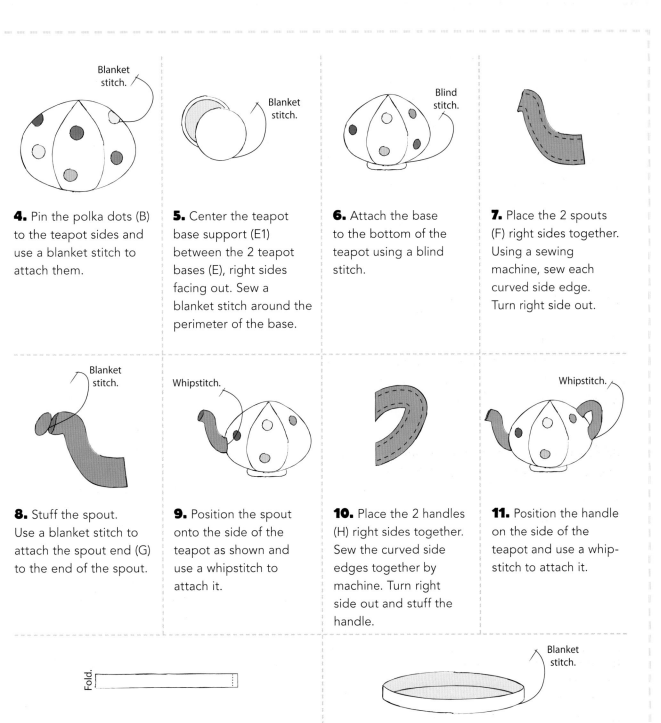

4. Pin the polka dots (B) to the teapot sides and use a blanket stitch to attach them.

5. Center the teapot base support (E1) between the 2 teapot bases (E), right sides facing out. Sew a blanket stitch around the perimeter of the base.

6. Attach the base to the bottom of the teapot using a blind stitch.

7. Place the 2 spouts (F) right sides together. Using a sewing machine, sew each curved side edge. Turn right side out.

8. Stuff the spout. Use a blanket stitch to attach the spout end (G) to the end of the spout.

9. Position the spout onto the side of the teapot as shown and use a whipstitch to attach it.

10. Place the 2 handles (H) right sides together. Sew the curved side edges together by machine. Turn right side out and stuff the handle.

11. Position the handle on the side of the teapot and use a whipstitch to attach it.

12. Fold the teapot lid side (D) in half right sides together. Sew the short ends together by machine. Turn right side out.

13. Place the teapot lid side (D) around a teapot lid (C) with wrong sides together. Use a blanket stitch to sew around the perimeter to attach the pieces, forming the lid bottom.

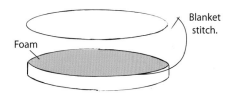

Foam

Blanket stitch.

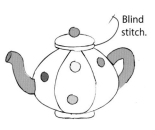

Blind stitch.

14. Insert the teapot lid foam circle (C) into the bottom of the teapot lid. Place a felt teapot lid (C) on top of the foam and stitch around the perimeter with a blanket stitch. Before closing the top, add a bit of stuffing to round out the top of the lid.

15. Use a blind stitch to attach the teapot lid to the top of the teapot.

16. Use a blind stitch to attach the felt ball to the top of the teapot lid.

Teacup Assembly

Blanket stitch.

1. Following the fusible manufacturer's directions, fuse a teacup base support (J1), centered, between 2 teacup bases (J), with right sides of the felt facing out. Set aside.

2. Center the teacup side support (I1) on the wrong side of a teacup side (I) and fuse in place. To make the teacup more decorative, add the stripes to the right side of the teacup side (I) without interfacing before assembly.

3. Fold the teacup side (I) with fused interfacing in half, right sides together. Sew the short ends together by machine. Repeat with the teacup side (I) without interfacing, turning this piece right side out after stitching.

4. Slip the teacup side (I) with fused interfacing inside of the teacup side (I) without interfacing, wrong sides facing. Blanket stitch around the perimeter of the top edge.

Blanket stitch.

Whipstitch.

5. Use a blanket stitch to attach the teacup base to the bottom of the teacup.

6. Place the teacup handles (K) right sides together. Sew the inner curved edge by machine. Turn right side out.

7. Beginning at the bottom, stitch the outer curved edge of the handle together with a blanket stitch, leaving the ends open and adding stuffing as you sew up the side.

8. Position the handle on the side of the teacup. Secure the handle at the top and bottom openings with a whipstitch to complete the teacup.

9. Follow Steps 1–8 to complete the other teacup.

Flower Crown

A crown is a necessity to feel like royalty at any tea party! Envision this crown of flowers on your little one—barefoot, spinning in circles with her favorite stuffed friends at her backyard tea party.

MATERIALS • Makes one flower crown.

Patterns can be found on page CD13.

Material	Amount	Cut
Red felt	9″ × 12″	Cut 6 small geranium petals (A), 8 large geranium petals (B), and 2 crown bases (L).
Purple felt	9″ × 12″	Cut 1 zinnia (C) and 1 flower center (E).
Orange felt	9″ × 12″	Cut 10 daisy petals (F) and 1 flower center (E).
Yellow felt	9″ × 12″	Cut 1 coneflower (D) and 2 flower centers (E).
Pink felt	9″ × 12″	Cut 5 small rose petals (G), 7 large rose petals (H), 1 rose center (I), and 1 flower center (E).
Aqua felt	9″ × 12″	Cut 5 pansy petals (M) and 1 coneflower (D).
Dark green felt	9″ × 12″	Cut 2 small leaves (J) and 3 large leaves (K).
Kelly green felt	9″ × 12″	Cut 3 small leaves (J).
Embroidery floss—red, purple, orange, yellow, pink, teal, green		
Yarn	3 yards	Cut 6 sections 18″ long.

Flower Crown Assembly

1. Tie a knot at the base of a strand of embroidery floss. Stitch through the bottom of a red small geranium petal (A).

2. Repeat, moving the needle through each of the 6 small geranium petals (A). After you have sewn through all the petals, gently pull the thread taut and tie a knot. Repeat with the 8 red large geranium petals (B). Repeat with 5 aqua pansy petals (M).

3. Starting at an end, roll up a yellow flower center (E). Make small stitches in the bottom to secure it. Make 2.

4. Place the small red geranium cluster on top of the large red geranium cluster and secure them together with stitches.

5. Place a yellow flower center in the center of the red geranium petals and use small stitches to secure it. Set aside.

6. Repeat Step 5 with the aqua pansy cluster and the other yellow center. Set aside.

7. Fold the purple zinnia (C) in half lengthwise. Use a basting stitch along the bottom open edge to secure the 2 sides together. Make clips with scissors along the folded edge about ½″ apart and ½″ deep.

← Roll.

8. Beginning at an end, roll up the purple zinnia (C). Make small stitches at the bottom to secure it. Set aside.

9. Overlap the straight sides of the yellow coneflower (D). Use a running stitch to secure the sides together.

10. Create a pink flower center (E) following the directions in Step 3.

11. Place the pink flower center in the center of the yellow coneflower and use small stitches to secure it. Set aside.

12. Follow Steps 9–11 to create an aqua coneflower (D) with an orange flower center (E). Set aside.

13. Tie a knot at the base of a strand of embroidery floss. Stitch through the bottom of an orange daisy petal (F).

14. Repeat, moving the needle through each of the daisy petals (F). After you have sewn through all 10 petals, pull the thread taut and tie a knot.

15. Repeat Step 3 to create a purple flower center (E). Secure the flower center to the center of the daisy with small stitches.

← Roll.

16. Tie a knot at the base of a strand of embroidery floss. Stitch through the bottom of a pink small rose petal (G).

17. Repeat, moving the needle through each of the small rose petals (G). After you have sewn through all the petals, pull the thread taut and tie a knot. Repeat with all of the large rose petals (H).

18. Repeat Step 3 to create the pink rose center (I).

19. Place the small rose into the large rose and stitch in place. Place the rose center into the small petals and secure with stitches. Set aside.

20. On a dark green small leaf (J), sew a straight stitch down the center by machine. I used a contrasting thread to pop out against the dark green. Make 2. Set aside.

21. Layer a kelly green small leaf (J) over the dark green large leaf (K). Use a decorative zigzag stitch to sew down the center of the leaf by machine. Repeat to create 2 more leaves.

22. Arrange the flowers as you wish on the right side of a crown base (L) and pin into place. Use a needle and thread to secure the flowers to the base.

23. Tuck the leaves into the ends and secure those with a needle and thread.

24. Create 2 braids with the 6 yarn segments and tie off ends. Sew a length of braided yarn to each end of the wrong side of the other crown base (L) by machine.

25. Place the crown base with attached flowers on top of the crown base with yarn, wrong sides together. Blanket stitch around the perimeter to complete the flower crown.

We All Scream for Ice Cream!

Some of my most poignant childhood memories revolve around ice cream. These memories range from the ice cream truck that would drive through my neighborhood to the retro diner we would go to for chili cheese fries and ice cream sodas after a night at the roller skating rink. Ice cream was always such a special treat.

Scoop of Ice Cream

MATERIALS • **Makes one scoop of ice cream.**

Patterns can be found on page CD14.

Material	Amount	Cut
Pink felt	9″ × 12″	Cut 2 scoop bases (A) and 1 scoop top (B).
Embroidery floss—pink		
Stuffing		

Scoop of Ice Cream Assembly

Leave opening.

1. Place 2 scoop bases (A) right sides together. Sew around the perimeter by machine, leaving an opening to turn right side out.

Blind stitch.

2. Turn the scoop base (A) right side out. Stuff the scoop base (A) and blindstitch the opening closed. Set aside.

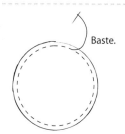

Baste.

3. With the wrong side up, run a basting stitch around the scoop top (B).

4. Begin to add stuffing as you pull the thread taut on the scoop top (B). Tie a knot to secure the thread once the scoop top (B) is fully stuffed.

Blind stitch.

5. Place the scoop top (B) over the scoop base (A). Blindstitch around the base of the scoop top (B) to secure it to the scoop base (A). This will complete the scoop of ice cream.

Ice Cream Scooper

MATERIALS • Makes one ice cream scooper.

Patterns can be found on page CD15.

Material	Amount	Cut
Gray felt	9″ × 12″	Cut 12 scooper sides (A).
Pink felt	4″ × 6″	Cut 1 handle side (B) and 1 handle end (C).
Heavyweight fusible interfacing	6″ × 10″	Cut 6 scooper side supports (A1).
Embroidery floss—gray, pink		
Stuffing		

Ice Cream Scooper Assembly

1. Following the manufacturer's instructions, fuse the 6 scooper side supports (A1) to the wrong side of 6 scooper sides (A).

2. Place 2 interfaced scooper sides (A) right sides together. Sew 1 curved edge by machine. Continue adding remaining interfaced scooper sides (A) until you have connected 6 scooper sides in a row. Sew the first and last sides to form a bowl shape. Turn right side out.

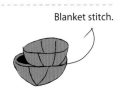

Blanket stitch.

3. Repeat Step 2 with remaining scooper sides (A), creating another bowl shape. Leave this bowl with the seams facing out.

4. Place the scooper without the interfacing inside of the scooper with interfacing. Make sure the wrong sides are facing and take care to align the seams. Pin the top to secure it.

5. Sew around the top perimeter with a blanket stitch. Set aside.

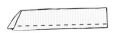

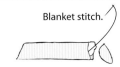

Blanket stitch.

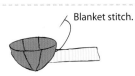

Blanket stitch.

6. Fold the handle side (B) in half lengthwise, right sides together. Sew the long edges together by machine. Turn right side out.

7. Use a blanket stitch to attach the handle end (C) to the bottom of the handle side. Stuff the handle and finish attaching the end.

8. Position the angled end of the handle (B) on the side of the scooper (A) and attach it with a blanket stitch to complete the scooper.

Hot Fudge Sundae

MATERIALS • Makes one ice cream sundae.

Patterns can be found on page CD16.

Material	Amount	Cut
White felt	9″ × 12″	Cut 1 whipped cream (D), 1 scoop of ice cream top (B, page CD14), and 2 scoop of ice cream bases (A, page CD14).
Gray felt	9″ × 12″	Cut 14 cup sides (A) and 2 cup bottoms (B).
Brown felt	5″ × 5″	Cut 1 hot fudge (C).
Red felt	3″ × 3″	Cut 1 cherry (E).
Tan felt	3″ × 3″	Cut ⅛″ × ⅛″ squares for chopped nuts.
Ivory felt	3″ × 3″	Cut ⅛″ × ⅛″ squares for chopped nuts.
fast2fuse heavy double-sided stiff fusible inter-facing	8″ × 8″	Cut 7 cup side supports (A1) and 1 cup bottom support (B1).
Embroidery floss—gray, white, brown, red, tan		
Stuffing		

Hot Fudge Sundae Assembly

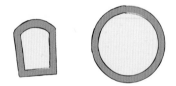

1. Following the manufacturer's instructions, fuse a cup side support (A1) to the wrong side of a cup side (A). Repeat with remaining 6 cup side supports. Fuse cup bottom support (B1) to wrong side of cup bottom (B).

2. Fuse a plain cup side (A) to an interfaced cup side (A), wrong sides together. Repeat with remaining 6 cup side (A) pairs. Fuse the plain cup bottom (B) to the interfaced cup bottom (B), wrong sides together. Set aside.

Blanket stitch.

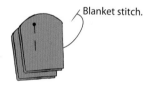

3. Place 2 fused cup sides (A) together, and stitch together along 1 side using a blanket stitch.

Blanket stitch.

4. Continue adding remaining fused cup sides (A) until you have connected 7 sides and formed a cup shape.

5. Use a blanket stitch to attach the fused cup bottom (B) to the attached cup sides (A). Blanket stitch along top edges of cup.

6. Create a scoop of ice cream following the directions in Scoop of Ice Cream (page 28).

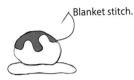

7. Use a blanket stitch to attach the hot fudge (C) to the top of the scoop of ice cream.

8. Make small stitches to attach the small tan and ivory felt squares (nuts) on top of the hot fudge (C).

9. Make the whipped cream (D) (see Cake Assembly in the Sweetie Pie Bakery section, Steps 6–9, page 104). Use a blind stitch to attach the whipped cream to the top of the hot fudge (C).

10. To create the cherry (E), sew a gathering stitch around the perimeter of the cherry (E), with the wrong side facing up.

11. As you begin to pull the thread taut, add stuffing to the cherry (E).

12. After the cherry (E) is stuffed, tie a knot to secure.

13. For the stem, stitch 6 strands of embroidery floss through the top of the cherry (E).

14. Holding the strands together, braid the floss together, and then tie a knot at the end.

15. Use a blind stitch to attach the cherry (E) to the top of the whipped cream (D) to complete the hot fudge sundae.

Ice Cream Cookie

MATERIALS • Makes one ice cream cookie.

Patterns can be found on page CD17.

Material	Amount	Cut
Tan felt	9″ × 12″	Cut 4 cookie bases (A).
White felt	9″ × 12″	Cut 1 ice cream side (C) and 2 ice cream bases (B).
½″-thick foam	5″ × 5″	Cut 1 ice cream base (B).
½″ buttons—brown	6	
Embroidery floss—tan, white		
Stuffing		

Ice Cream Cookie Assembly

Leave opening.

1. Place 2 of the cookie bases (A) right sides together. Machine sew around the cookie base (A), leaving a small opening. Turn right side out.

2. Stuff the cookie base (A) with a small amount of stuffing, and then blindstitch the opening closed.

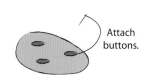

Attach buttons.

3. Use a needle and thread to attach 3 buttons to the top of the cookie.

4. Repeat Steps 1–3 to complete another cookie base.

5. To make the ice cream, fold the ice cream side (C) in half, right sides together. Machine sew the short ends together. Turn right side out.

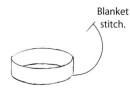

Blanket stitch.

6. Place an ice cream base (B) and the ice cream side (C) wrong sides together. Use a blanket stitch to stitch around the perimeter to connect the pieces.

Blanket stitch.

Foam

7. Insert the foam into the ice cream base (C) with attached side. Place the other ice cream base (C) on top and blanket stitch around the perimeter.

Blind stitch.

8. Place a cookie base (A) on top of the ice cream, with the buttons facing up. Blindstitch the bottom of the cookie base to the top of the ice cream. Repeat with the other cookie base on the bottom of the ice cream to complete the ice cream cookie sandwich.

Ice Cream Sandwich

MATERIALS • Makes one ice cream sandwich.

Patterns can be found on page CD18.

Material	Amount	Cut
Dark brown felt	9″ × 12″	Cut 4 sandwich cookies (A).
White felt	9″ × 12″	Cut 1 ice cream side (C) and 1 ice cream top (B).
½″-thick foam	5″ × 5″	Cut 1 ice cream top (B).
Embroidery floss—brown, white		
Stuffing		

Ice Cream Sandwich Assembly

Leave opening.

1. Place 2 of the sandwich cookies (A) right sides together. Machine sew around the sandwich cookie (A), leaving a small opening to turn right side out.

2. Stuff the sandwich cookie (A) with a small amount of stuffing, and then blindstitch the opening closed.

French knots

3. Referring to the pattern, stitch French knots to the top of the sandwich cookie (A), stitching through all layers.

4. Repeat Steps 1–3 to complete another sandwich cookie.

5. To create the ice cream, follow Steps 5–7 in Ice Cream Cookie Assembly (page 32).

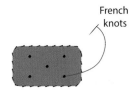

Blind stitch.

6. With the French knots facing up, place a sandwich cookie (A) on top of the ice cream. Blindstitch the bottom of the sandwich cookie (A) to the top of the ice cream. Repeat with the other sandwich cookie (A) on the bottom of the ice cream to complete the ice cream sandwich.

Sugar Cone

MATERIALS • Makes one sugar cone. See Scoop of Ice Cream (page 28) to make one or more scoops of ice cream.

Patterns can be found on page CD19.

Material	Amount	Cut
Tan felt	9″ × 12″	Cut 1 sugar cone (A) and 1 sugar cone top (B).
Heavyweight fusible interfacing	4″ × 4″	Cut 1 sugar cone top support (B1).
Embroidery floss—brown, white		
Stuffing		

Sugar Cone Assembly

1. With the right side of the sugar cone (A) facing up, machine sew the diagonal lines ½″ apart as indicated on the pattern. Machine sew the diagonal lines that run in the other direction.

2. Following the manufacturer's directions, fuse the sugar cone top support interfacing (B1) to the wrong side of the sugar cone top (B).

3. Fold the cone (A) in half, right sides together. Sew the straight edge by machine. Turn right side out.

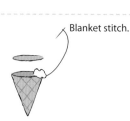

Blanket stitch.

4. Stuff the sugar cone (A). Place the sugar cone top (B) over the stuffing and use a blanket stitch to attach the top to the cone.

Blind stitch.

5. Use a blind stitch to attach the base of a scoop of ice cream to the cone top—or add 3 to make a triple scoop!

Ice Cream Bar

MATERIALS • Makes one ice cream bar.

Patterns can be found on page CD20.

Material	Amount	Cut
Orange felt	9″ × 12″	Cut 2 (1 and 1 reversed) bars (A), 1 bar side 1 (B), and 1 bar side 2 (D).
White felt	3″ × 4″	Cut 1 rectangle 1″ × 1⅝″ for bar bite (C) and 1 rectangle 1″ × 2¾″ for bar bottom (E).
Tan felt	3″ × 3″	Cut 2 sticks (F).
1″-thick foam		Cut 1 bar (A).
Small Popsicle stick		
Embroidery floss— orange, white, tan		

Ice Cream Bar Assembly

Blanket stitch.

1. Place bar side 1 (B) and bar bite (C) right sides together. Using a sewing machine, sew the short ends together.

2. Align bar side 2 (D) with the other end of the bite (C), right sides together. Use a sewing machine to sew the short ends together.

3. Pin the attached sides around the side of the foam bar. Place a bar (A) on top.

4. Use a blanket stitch to attach the bar (A) to the bar side pieces.

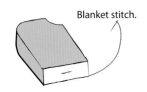

Blanket stitch.

Blanket stitch.

Blanket stitch.

5. Cut a slit in the bar bottom (E) as indicated on the pattern. Place the bar bottom (E) over the bottom of the foam and attach it with a blanket stitch.

6. Use a hand-held cutting tool to create a slit in the bottom of the foam bar. Set aside.

7. Place the 2 sticks (F) wrong sides together. Use a blanket stitch to stitch around the perimeter, leaving the top open. Slide the Popsicle stick inside.

8. Slide the stick into the slit in the bar bottom (E). Use a blanket stitch to stitch around the perimeter of the stick and bar opening to complete the ice cream bar.

Ice Cream Container

MATERIALS • Makes one ice cream container.

Patterns can be found on pages CD21–CD27.

Material	Amount	Cut
White felt	¼ yard	Cut 2 container sides (E), 2 container bottoms (F), and 1 circle 1½" for inner logo (D).
Pink felt	⅓ yard	Cut 4 rectangles 1¾" × 5" for container stripes (I), 2 circles 4¾" for lid top (G), 2 rectangles 1" × 15⅜" for lid sides (H), 1 ice cream side (A), and 2 circles 4⅜" for ice cream bases (B). Cut ice cream shapes for inner logo (D) from leftover pink felt.
Dark brown felt	3" × 3"	Cut 1 circle 2" for outer logo (C).
Tan felt	1" × 1"	Cut 1 cone shape (see pattern D) for inner logo.
Heavyweight fusible interfacing	¼ yard	Cut 1 rectangle 4½" × 14" for container side support (E1), 1 rectangle ½" × 14" for lid side support (H1), 1 circle 4" for container bottom support (F1), and 1 lid support (G1).
Embroidery floss—white, tan, pink, brown		
Stuffing		

Ice Cream Assembly

1. Fold the ice cream side (A) in half, right sides together. Sew the short ends together by machine. Turn right side out.

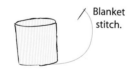

Blanket stitch.

2. Use a blanket stitch to attach an ice cream base (B) to the ice cream side (A).

Blind stitch.

3. Stuff the ice cream. Place the other ice cream base (B) over the stuffing and secure with a blanket stitch. Before closing the circle, add enough stuffing to fill the ice cream. Set aside.

Container Assembly

1. Use a running stitch to sew the ice cream cone shapes on the inner logo circle (D). Center the inner logo circle on top of the outer logo (C) and attach with a running stitch. Set aside.

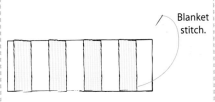

Blanket stitch.

2. Use a blanket stitch to secure the container stripes (I) to a container side (E).

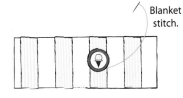

Blanket stitch.

3. Use a blanket stitch to secure the completed logo to the container side (E), centering it over a middle stripe.

4. Fold a container side (E) in half, right sides together. Sew the ends together. Turn right side out.

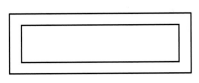

5. Following the manufacturer's instructions, fuse the container side support (E1) to the wrong side of the other container side (E). Fold the interfaced container side (E) in half, right sides together. Sew the ends together. Do not turn right side out.

6. Slide the interfaced container side, with seams out, inside the container side with attached logo and stripes, taking care to align seams. Set aside.

7. Following the manufacturer's instructions, fuse the container bottom support (F1) to the wrong side of a container bottom (F). Pin the other container bottom (F) on top with right side facing up.

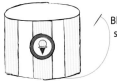

Blanket stitch.

8. Using a blanket stitch, stitch around the perimeter of the container bottom (F), attaching it to the container side (E), stitching through all 4 layers of felt.

9. Using a blanket stitch, stitch around the perimeter of the top of the container side (E).

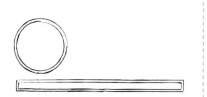

Rickrack

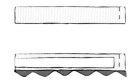

10. Following the manufacturer's instructions, center and fuse the lid side support (H1) to the wrong side of a lid side (H). Fuse the lid support (G1) to the wrong side of a lid top (G). Pin the other lid top (G) on top with right side facing up. Set aside.

11. Place the rickrack in position on the interfaced lid side (H) and machine sew in place.

12. Fold both lid sides (H) in half, right sides together. Using a sewing machine, sew the short ends together. Turn right side out.

Running stitch

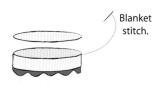

Blanket stitch.

Attach lid top.

13. Slide the lid side (H) with attached interfacing inside of the other lid side (H). Take care to align the seams. Use a running stitch to sew around the perimeter of the lid side, through the rickrack and all lid side layers.

14. To complete the lid, use a blanket stitch to stitch around the perimeter, connecting the lid top (G) and lid side (H).

15. Insert the ice cream into the container and place the lid on top of the container.

Take Me Out to the Ballgame

Ballgames are an all-American pastime. As a family, we love spending time together at summer baseball games, cheering on our Chicago Cubbies, indulging in treats, and creating memories together. This set was inspired by memories we've made and wish to continue to make as a family. My children also enjoy re-creating these memories themselves; by watching them play, I was inspired to create this playset just for them.

Caramel Corn

MATERIALS • Makes one box of caramel corn.

Patterns can be found on pages CD28 and CD29.

Material	Amount	Cut
White felt	2 sheets 9″ × 12″	Cut 4 box fronts (B), 2 box hinges (D), 6 box bases (E), and 4 box sides (F).
Red felt	9″ × 12″	Cut 1 caramel corn logo (A).
Tan felt	9″ × 12″	Cut 3 caramel corns (C).
Ivory felt	9″ × 12″	Cut 3 caramel corns (C).
fast2fuse heavy double-sided stiff interfacing	7″ × 7″	Cut 2 box front supports (B1), 3 box base supports (E1), and 2 box side supports (F1).
Hook-and-loop tape, white, ⅝″ wide	2″	
Embroidery floss—white, red, tan		
Stuffing		

Caramel Corn and Box Assembly

Baste raw edge.

Roll.

1. Place 2 caramel corn (C) strips right sides together. I alternated colors, using a tan and an ivory together. Using a sewing machine, sew a long side together. Trim the seam.

2. Turn right side out and sew a basting stitch on the other long bottom edge.

3. Cut the caramel corn (C) into 2½″ sections and then make slits in the top (about 5 or 6 slits per section). Repeat for the rest of the caramel corn (C). Don't cut through the basting stitches.

4. Starting at an end, begin to roll up a caramel corn (C) section and make stitches in the base to secure it. Repeat Steps 1–3 for all of the caramel corn (C) sections. Make sure to alternate the tan on the outside of the caramel corn and the ivory on the outside to add variety. Set aside.

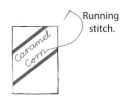

Running stitch.

5. Following the manufacturer's instructions, center and fuse the support pieces B1, E1, and F1 to the wrong side of the corresponding felt pieces B, E, and F. Fuse the remaining E and F felt pieces to the wrong sides of the corresponding interfaced pieces.

6. Place the box logo (A) on the box front (B) without interfacing. Attach the logo using a running stitch. Set aside.

7. Cut a 2″ strip of hook-and-loop tape. Separate the hook side from the loop side. Sew the hook side to the right side of a fused box base (E), using a short stitch on the sewing machine.

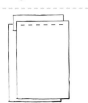

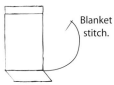

Blanket stitch.

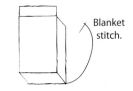

Blanket stitch.

8. To assemble the hinge (D), place 2 box fronts (B) wrong sides together. Slip the hinge (D) between the top edge of the box fronts by ½″. Fuse together. Machine sew on top of the box front (B) with a narrow seam, connecting the hinge (D) into the box fronts (B). Repeat to make another box front (B) with hinge.

9. Place a box front (B) and a box base (E) together, aligning the edges. Stitch with a blanket stitch to attach the 2 box pieces.

10. When you reach the corner, add the box side (F), and so on, continuing around the base (E).

Blanket stitch.

Blanket stitch.

11. After you have sewn on the box fronts (B) and box sides (F), stitch each corner using a blanket stitch, a corner at a time.

12. Place a box base (E) on either side of a hinge (D). Use a blanket stitch to attach the box base to the hinge. Sew along the bottom edge on both sides of the hinge and all around the perimeter of the base. Repeat with the other hinge, making sure that the side of the base with the hook tape is facing the inside of the box.

13. Fill the box with caramel corn to complete the treat.

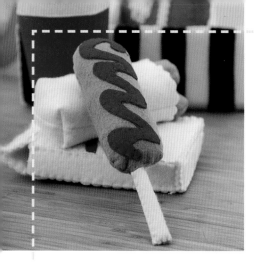

Corn Dog

MATERIALS • Makes one corn dog.

Patterns can be found on page CD30.

Material	Amount	Cut
Tan felt	9″ × 12″	Cut 2 corn dog pieces (B).
Ivory felt	2″ × 5″	Cut 1 corn dog stick (A).
Red felt	3″ × 5″	Cut 1 condiment piece (C).
Yellow felt (*optional*)	3″ × 5″	Cut 1 condiment piece (C) (*optional*).
Dowel rod, ⅜″ diameter	5″ long	
Embroidery floss—ivory, red, yellow (*optional*)		
Stuffing		

Corn Dog Assembly

1. Place the corn dog pieces (B) right sides together. Sew around the perimeter, leaving a 1½″ opening at the bottom.

2. Clip the curves and turn the corn dog (B) right side out.

3. Stuff the corn dog (B). Set aside.

Blanket stitch.

4. Fold the corn dog stick (A) lengthwise, wrong sides together. Blanket stitch around the perimeter to join the raw edges, leaving the top open. Slip in the dowel rod.

5. Slip the corn dog stick (A) into the opening of the corn dog (B).

Blind stitch.

6. Using a blind stitch, sew the corn dog stick (A) to the base of the corn dog (B) to secure it, and then sew the seam allowance closed.

Blanket stitch.

7. Use a blanket stitch to attach the condiments (C) (ketchup and optional mustard) to the top of the corn dog (B).

Cotton Candy

MATERIALS • Makes one cotton candy.

Patterns can be found on page CD31.

Material	Amount	Cut
White felt	9″ × 12″	Cut 1 handle (A).
Pink felt	2 sheets 9″ × 12″	Cut 2 cotton candy (B).
Pink wool roving	About 0.1 oz.	
Embroidery floss—white, pink		
Stuffing		

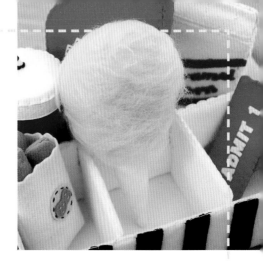

Cotton Candy Assembly

1. Use a sewing machine to sew the white diagonal lines as provided on the handle (A) pattern template.

2. Fold the handle (A) in half, right sides together. Sew the sides together, leaving the top open, and turn right side out. Stuff the handle (A). Set aside.

3. Place the cotton candy pieces (B) right sides together. Sew around the perimeter, leaving a 2″ opening to turn right side out.

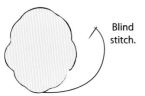

4. Clip the curves and turn right side out. Stuff the cotton candy and blindstitch the opening closed.

5. Set the cotton candy (B) over the handle (A). Blanket stitch around the perimeter of the top of the handle (A) to secure the handle (A) to the cotton candy (B).

6. Pull the roving apart so that it is still connected but you can see light through it. Wrap it around the cotton candy (B) a few times to complete it. The roving will naturally secure itself.

Peanuts

MATERIALS • Makes five peanuts and one bag.

Patterns can be found on page CD32.

Material	Amount	Cut
Light blue felt	3″ × 3″	Cut 1 logo circle (A).
Tan felt	9″ × 12″	Cut 1 logo peanut (A) and 10 peanuts (C).
White felt	9″ × 12″	Cut 2 peanut bags (B).
Embroidery floss—navy, tan, white		
Stuffing		
Pinking shears or pinking blade and rotary cutter		

Peanut and Bag Assembly

Running stitch.

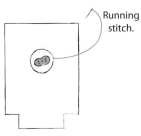

Running stitch.

Running stitch.

1. Use small stitches on the logo peanut (A) to attach it to the logo circle (A).

2. Use a running stitch to attach the logo (A) to a peanut bag (B).

3. Place both peanut bags (B) right sides together. Sew down both sides, ending the stitching at the cutouts. Then stitch across the bottom of the bag.

4. Open the corners and align the side and bottom seams. Sew across the corners. Turn the bag right side out.

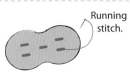

Running stitch.

5. Trim the top of the bag with pinking shears or a pinking blade on a rotary cutter. Set aside.

6. Using embroidery floss, make small stitches on a peanut (C) as indicated on the pattern.

7. Place 2 peanuts (C) right sides together, pairing a stitched peanut with a plain one. Sew around the perimeter, leaving an opening to turn the peanut right side out.

8. Turn the peanut right side out, stuff the peanut, and blindstitch the opening closed.

9. Repeat Steps 6–8 to make a total of 5 peanuts.

10. Fill the peanut bag (B) with the peanuts.

Popsicle

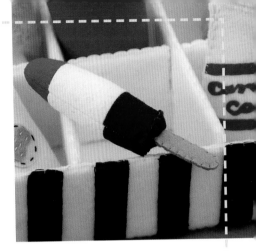

MATERIALS • Makes one Popsicle.

Patterns can be found on page CD33.

Material	Amount	Cut
Red felt	9″ × 12″	Cut 2 Popsicle sections (B).
White felt	9″ × 12″	Cut 2 Popsicle sections (B).
Blue felt	9″ × 12″	Cut 2 Popsicle sections (B) and 1 Popsicle bottom (C).
Tan felt	4″ × 4″	Cut 2 sticks (A).
Small wooden Popsicle stick		
Embroidery floss—tan and blue		
Stuffing		

Popsicle Assembly

Blanket stitch.

1. Place the Popsicle sticks (A) wrong sides together. Blanket stitch around the perimeter to secure them, leaving the top open. Slip the wooden Popsicle stick into the sewn Popsicle stick (A). Set aside.

2. To assemble a Popsicle front, place a red and a white Popsicle section (B) right sides together. Sew the long edge by machine. Open up the sections (B) and sew the blue onto the white the same way. Repeat with the other Popsicle sections (B).

3. Place the sewn Popsicle sections right sides together, aligning the seams. Center the Popsicle front (D) pattern over the sewn Popsicle sections and cut out the 2 Popsicle fronts.

4. Place the front pieces right sides together and sew around the perimeter, leaving the bottom open. Turn right side out. Stuff the Popsicle.

Blanket stitch.

Blind stitch.

5. Cut a slit in the Popsicle bottom (C) piece as indicated on the pattern. Use a blanket stitch to attach the Popsicle bottom (C) to the bottom of the Popsicle.

6. Slip the Popsicle stick into the opening of the Popsicle bottom (C).

7. Leaving 2″ of Popsicle stick below the Popsicle bottom, attach the stick to the bottom using a blind stitch.

Foam Finger

MATERIALS • Makes one foam finger.

Patterns can be found on page CD34.

Material	Amount	Cut
White felt	9″ × 12″	Cut 1 finger logo (A).
Orange felt	¼ yard	Cut 4 (2 and 2 reversed) finger tops (B) and 2 finger bottoms (D). Cut 1 rectangle 1″ × 23⅓″ for finger side (C) (no pattern provided).
½″-thick foam	17″ × 22″	Cut 2 fingers (B).
Embroidery floss— blue and orange		

Foam Finger Assembly

Running stitch.

Baste.

Felt
Foam
Felt

1. Use a running stitch to attach the finger logo (A) to a finger top (B).

2. Prepare the halves of the foam finger. Layer a finger top (B), a piece of foam, and another finger top (B). To create the first unit, use a basting stitch around all sides and sew through all of the layers, securing the foam between the felt layers.

3. Repeat Step 2 to create the second unit, making sure that the logo (A) is on top and the index finger is to the right and will align with the first unit.

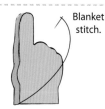

Blanket stitch.

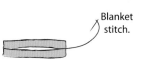

Blanket stitch.

4. Place the 2 pieces from Steps 2 and 3 together, making sure to align the corners and index fingers.

5. Pin the finger side (C) around the perimeter of the foam finger. Using a blanket stitch, sew around the top and side edges to attach the side (C) to the fingers (B).

6. Place a finger bottom (D) over the bottom of a finger half. Stitch around the perimeter with a blanket stitch. Repeat with the other half to complete the foam finger.

7. Remove any basting stitches from Step 2 that show.

Pennant

MATERIALS • Makes one pennant.

Patterns can be found on pages CD35–CD37.

Material	Amount	Cut
Blue felt	½ yard	Cut 2 pennants (B) and 1 dowel pocket (C).
White felt	9″ × 12″	Cut 1 pennant appliqué (A).
fast2fuse heavy double-sided stiff interfacing	8″ × 12″	Cut 1 pennant support (B1).
Dowel rod, ¼″ diameter	15″ long	
Embroidery floss—orange, navy		

Pennant Assembly

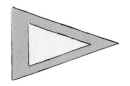

1. Following the manufacturer's instructions, center and fuse the interfacing support (B1) to the wrong side of a pennant (B) piece.

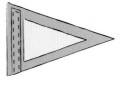

2. Place the dowel pocket (C) on the wrong side of the inter-faced pennant as indicated on the pattern template. Sew around the sides and top by machine. Leave the bottom of the pocket open, so that the dowel rod can slip into place.

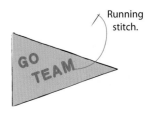

Running stitch.

3. Use a running stitch to attach the pennant appliqué (A) to the other pennant (B) piece.

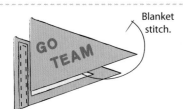

Blanket stitch.

4. Place the pennant (B) piece with attached appliqué (A) over the pennant (B) piece with the dowel pocket (C), with wrong sides together. Fuse together. Use a blanket stitch to stitch around the perimeter of the pennant. Take care not to close the opening where the dowel needs to slip in.

5. Slide the dowel rod in place to complete the pennant.

Tickets

MATERIALS • Makes two tickets.

Patterns can be found on page CD38.

Material	Amount	Cut
Orange felt	9″ × 12″	Cut 4 rectangles 2″ × 5″ for tickets (B).
White felt	9″ × 12″	Cut 2 ticket logos (A).
fast2fuse heavy double-sided stiff interfacing	4″ × 6″	Cut 2 rectangles 1½″ × 4½″ for ticket supports (B1).
Embroidery floss— orange, white		

Ticket Assembly

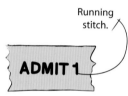

Running stitch.

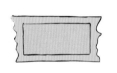

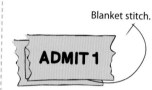

Blanket stitch.

1. Use a running stitch to attach a ticket logo (A) to the right side of a ticket (B).

2. Following the manufacturer's instructions, fuse a ticket support interfacing between a ticket with a logo and a ticket without a logo, wrong sides together.

3. Trim the ends with pinking shears or a rotary cutter with a scalloped blade, if you wish. Stitch around the perimeter with a blanket stitch.

4. Repeat Steps 1–3, creating another ticket.

Vendor Box

MATERIALS
Makes one vendor box.

Patterns can be found on pages CD39–CD44.

Material	Amount	Cut
Blue felt	2 sheets 9″ × 12″	Cut 21 vendor box stripes (A).
White felt, 40″ wide	1 yard	Cut 4 vendor box sides (B), 4 vendor box fronts (C), 4 grid tops (E), and 2 grid bases (F). Cut 2 rectangles 9″ × 12″ for vendor box bottom (D) (no pattern provided).
Foamcore board	1 sheet 26″ × 30″	Cut 2 box side supports (B1), 2 box front supports (C1), 2 grid top supports (E1), and 1 grid base support (F1). Cut 1 rectangle 8½″ × 11½″ for box bottom support (D1) (no pattern provided).
Grosgrain ribbon, 1½″ wide—orange	1½ yards	
Glue		
Embroidery floss—blue, white		

Vendor Box Assembly

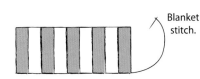

Blanket stitch.

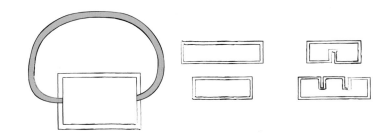

1. Use a blanket stitch to attach the vendor box stripes (A) to 2 of the vendor box sides (B) and 2 of the fronts (C), using the lines provided on the pattern for guidance. Space the blue stripes so they will alternate with white background when all 4 sides and fronts are joined.

2. Glue the foamcore board between the corresponding felt pieces for the box fronts (C), grid top (E), and grid base (F). Do not glue the foamcore board side supports (B1) to the felt sides (B) yet. When you glue the vendor box bottom (D) and bottom support (D1), slip the end of the ribbon between the felt and the board to secure it on each end. Add a foamcore board side support (B1) to each of 2 box sides (B), but do not glue a second felt box side (B) to either piece yet. The box sides will be sandwiched around the ribbon in Step 3.

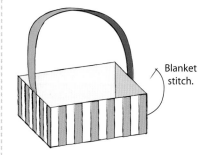

Blanket stitch.

Blanket stitch.

3. Position the vendor box front (C) on a long edge of the box bottom (D). Stitch along the bottom edge with a blanket stitch. Make sure to stitch through all 4 layers of felt. When you reach the corner, add the vendor box side (B), sandwiching the ribbon between the side pieces. Continue until you have gone all the way around the bottom of the box.

4. After you have secured the bottom perimeter of the box, stitch up each corner with a blanket stitch, a corner at a time.

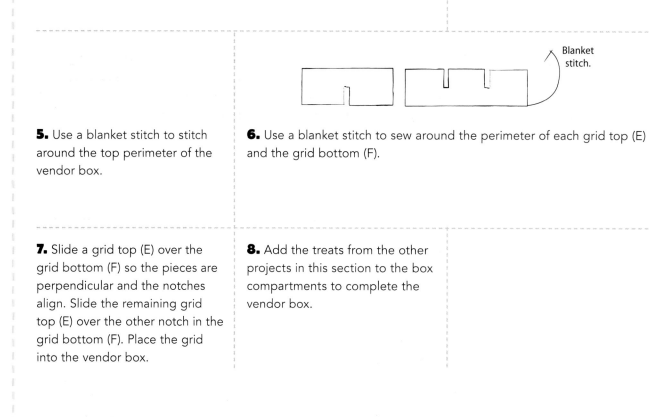

Blanket stitch.

5. Use a blanket stitch to stitch around the top perimeter of the vendor box.

6. Use a blanket stitch to sew around the perimeter of each grid top (E) and the grid bottom (F).

7. Slide a grid top (E) over the grid bottom (F) so the pieces are perpendicular and the notches align. Slide the remaining grid top (E) over the other notch in the grid bottom (F). Place the grid into the vendor box.

8. Add the treats from the other projects in this section to the box compartments to complete the vendor box.

Soda

MATERIALS • Makes one soda.

Patterns can be found on pages CD45 and CD46.

Material	Amount	Cut
Red felt	9″ × 12″	Cut 1 soda side (B) and 1 soda bottom (C).
White felt	9″ × 12″	Cut 1 lid strip (A), 1 soda lid (D), and 1 straw (E).
Blue felt	1″ × 6″	Cut 1 straw detail (F).
Heavyweight fusible interfacing	¼ yard	Cut 1 soda bottom support (C1) and 1 soda lid support (D1).
Pipe cleaner	1	Cut 1 piece 2¾″ long.
Embroidery floss—red, white		
Stuffing		

Soda Assembly

1. Place the lid strip (A) over the top of the soda side (B). Stitch using a sewing machine or use a blanket stitch along the bottom edge to secure it.

2. Fold the soda side from Step 1 in half, right sides together. Sew the long edge together by machine. Turn right side out.

3. Following the manufacturer's instructions, fuse the interfacing to the wrong side of the soda bottom (C) and soda lid (D).

4. Use a blanket stitch to attach the soda bottom (C) to the bottom of the soda.

5. Stuff the soda with stuffing.

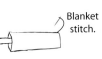

6. Place the soda lid (D) over the stuffing and stitch around the perimeter with a blanket stitch. Before you close the opening, add enough stuffing to completely fill the soda.

7. Place the pipe cleaner in the center of the straw (E). Fold the straw (E) in half lengthwise, with wrong sides together, over the pipe cleaner. Use a blanket stitch to sew around the end and the long side of the straw.

8. Wrap the straw detail (F) around the straw, securing the top and bottom with a few stitches with a needle and thread.

9. Place the straw (E) into the opening in the soda lid (D). Use a whipstitch to secure the straw (E) in the opening. Bend the straw to complete the soda.

Grill Master

This pattern is fun for any little grill master! When the weather finally warms up here in Wisconsin, we like to enjoy as much of it as we can. This means that most of our meals are prepared outdoors. My children enjoy grilling along with Dad, serving up their finest version of a T-bone steak.

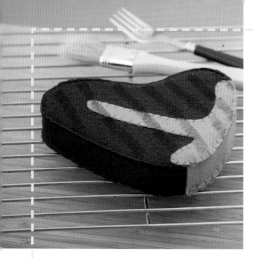

Steak

MATERIALS • Makes one steak.

Patterns can be found on page CD47.

Material	Amount	Cut
Dark brown felt	¼ yard	Cut 2 steak bases (B) and 1 steak side (C).
Tan felt	9″ × 12″	Cut 2 bone tops (A) and 1 bone side (D).
1″-wide foam	6″ × 6″	Cut 1 steak base (B).
Embroidery floss—dark brown, tan		
Black permanent marker		

Steak Assembly

Blanket stitch.

1. Using a blanket stitch, attach a bone top (A) to a steak base (B) with right sides up.

2. Repeat with the other steak base (B) and bone top (A). Make sure that they are mirrored, so the sides will be aligned when stacked. Set aside.

3. Lay the bone side (D) on an end of the steak side (C), with right sides together. Sew the short ends together on a sewing machine.

4. Join the 2 short ends of the piece from Step 3 together by machine, forming a circle. Turn right side out.

Blanket stitch.

5. Position the assembled steak side piece over a steak base (B) with attached bone top (A). Take care to align the bone side (D) with the attached bone top (A). With wrong sides together, stitch around the base with a blanket stitch to attach them.

6. Insert the foam steak support.

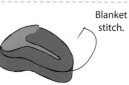

Blanket stitch.

7. Position the remaining steak base (B) over the foam support, and blanket stitch around the edge.

8. Add grill marks as shown in the photo (above) using a black permanent marker to complete the steak.

Kabob

MATERIALS • Makes one kabob set.

Patterns can be found on page CD48.

Material	Amount	Cut
Tan felt	9″ × 12″	Cut 1 skewer cover (A).
Brown felt	9″ × 12″	Cut 2 steak tops (C), 1 steak core (B), and 1 steak side (D).
Yellow felt	9″ × 12″	Cut 2 pineapple tops (F), 1 pineapple core (E), and 1 pineapple side (G).
Red felt	9″ × 12″	Cut 2 chili pepper tops (I), 1 chili pepper core (H), and 1 chili pepper side (J).
White felt	9″ × 12″	Cut 3 veggie slices (L).
Kelly green felt	4″ × 4″	Cut 1 chili pepper stem (K).
Burgundy felt	4″ × 4″	Cut 1 veggie slice (L).
Dowel rod, ¼″ diameter	8″ long	
Stuffing		
Embroidery floss—tan, light brown, yellow, red, white, green, burgundy		

Kabob Assembly

Blanket stitch.

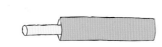

1. Fold the skewer cover (A) in half lengthwise, wrong sides together. Beginning at the bottom corner near the fold, stitch around the perimeter with a blanket stitch.

2. After you have stitched up the long side, insert the dowel rod and close the top to complete the skewer.

3. Fold the steak core (B) in half, right sides together. Machine sew the long ends together. Trim the seam allowance close to stitching.

4. Insert the steak core (B) in the center of the steak top (C) and use a blanket stitch to sew around the perimeter, attaching the pieces.

5. Fold the steak side (D) in half, right sides together. Machine sew the short ends closed. Turn right side out.

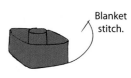

6. Position the steak side (D) around the steak top (C). Blanket stitch around the perimeter of the top (C).

7. Use a blanket stitch to stitch the other steak top (C) to the unit. Add stuffing as you work your way around to complete the steak cube.

8. Using yellow thread in the sewing machine, sew lines as indicated on the pattern of the pineapple side (G) to create the ridges of the pineapple slice. Set aside.

9. Follow Steps 3–7 to assemble the pineapple, using pieces E, F, and G.

10. Follow Steps 3–7 using pieces H, I, and J to assemble the chili pepper.

11. Roll up the chili pepper stem (K), beginning with a long side. Blanket stitch along the free edge to keep it closed.

12. Position the stem over the center back of the chili pepper and use a whipstitch to attach it.

13. Position a burgundy veggie slice (L) and a white veggie slice (L) wrong sides together. Using white thread in the sewing machine, sew lines ¼˝ apart on the burgundy veggie slice (L) to create the ridges in the red onion slice. Repeat with 2 white veggie slices (L) to create a white onion slice.

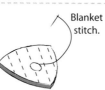

14. With white embroidery floss, blanket stitch around the interior and exterior perimeter of the veggie slice (L) to compete each onion slice.

15. Slide all of the pieces onto the skewer to complete the kabob.

Corn on the Cob

MATERIALS • **Makes one ear of corn on the cob.**

Patterns can be found on page CD49.

Material	Amount	Cut
Yellow felt	2 sheets 9″ × 12″	Cut 17 corn kernels (C).
White felt	9″ × 12″	Cut 2 corncob ends (A) and 1 corncob side (B).
Embroidery floss—yellow, white		
Stuffing		

Corn on the Cob Assembly

1. Using white thread in the sewing machine, sew the spiral pattern as indicated on the corncob end (A) pattern. Repeat on the other corncob end (A).

2. Fold the corncob side (B) in half, right sides together. Sew the short ends together. Turn right side out.

Blanket stitch.

3. With a blanket stitch, attach a corncob end (A) to the end of the corncob side (B).

4. Stuff the corncob with stuffing and attach the other corncob end (A) to the other end of the corncob. Set aside.

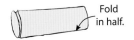

Fold in half.

5. Fold a corn kernel (C) in half, wrong sides together, so it measures about 1″ × 3″. Finger press to make a crease.

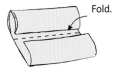

Fold.

6. Open the corn kernel (C) and fold the raw edges back in toward the crease you just made.

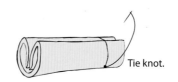

Tie knot.

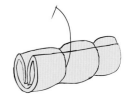

7. Fold the corn kernel (C) in half on the crease and pin down the strip.

8. Using a needle with yellow embroidery floss, tie a knot around the strip ¼˝ from the end.

9. Make 2 blind stitches in the seam of the strip and wrap the embroidery floss around the strip again, creating another kernel. Repeat this all the way down to create a row of 7 or 8 corn kernels (C).

Blind stitch.

10. Follow Steps 5–9 to create 16 more rows of corn kernels.

11. Using a blind stitch, attach each row to the corncob side (B) to complete the corn on the cob.

Watermelon

MATERIALS • Makes one watermelon slice.

Patterns can be found on page CD50.

Material	Amount	Cut
Red felt	9″ × 12″	Cut 2 melon bases (B) and 2 melon sides (E).
White felt	9″ × 12″	Cut 2 rind tops (C) and 2 rind top sides (F).
Kelly green felt	9″ × 12″	Cut 2 rind bottoms (D), 2 rind bottom sides (G), and 1 rind back (H).
Black felt	5″ × 5″	Cut 6 seeds (A).
1″ foam	6″ × 6″	
Embroidery floss—red, black, green		

Watermelon Assembly

1. Using black embroidery floss, blanket stitch 3 seeds (A) to a melon base (B). Repeat with the other melon base (B).

2. Position a melon base (B) with attached seeds (A) over the rind top (C). Align the edge of the melon base with the dashed line on the rind top (C). Topstitch the curved edge by machine. Trim the seam allowance on the back. Repeat to add the other rind top (C) to the remaining melon base (B).

3. Position the rind bottom (D) under the rind top (C), and topstitch the curved edge by machine. Trim the seam allowance on the back. Repeat to add rind bottom (D) to remaining piece from Step 2.

G F D

Blanket
stitch.

4. Repeat Steps 2 and 3 using pieces D, F, and G to assemble the sides of the watermelon.

5. Using the assembled watermelon base, trace a pattern for the foam insert, and cut out the foam.

6. Align the long edges of a watermelon base and a watermelon side. Stitch down the perimeter with a blanket stitch.

7. When you reach the tip of the watermelon, add the next side.

8. Continue working your way around the perimeter of the watermelon, finally adding the rind back (H).

9. Stitch up each corner in turn, using a blanket stitch.

Blanket
stitch.

10. Insert the 1″ foam into the base you just created.

11. Position the other melon base on top of the foam and blanket stitch around the upper perimeter to complete the watermelon.

Deviled Egg

MATERIALS • Makes one deviled egg.

Patterns can be found on page CD51.

Material	Amount	Cut
White felt	9″ × 12″	Cut 3 egg sides (A) and 1 egg top (B).
Pale yellow felt	9″ × 12″	Cut 1 filling (C).
Heavyweight fusible interfacing	3″ × 3″	Cut 1 egg top support (B1).
Embroidery floss—white, pale yellow		
Stuffing		

Deviled Egg Assembly

1. With right sides together, sew a curved edge of 2 egg sides (A) together by machine. Repeat to add the remaining egg side (A). Trim and turn right side out. Set aside.

2. Following the manufacturer's instructions, fuse the egg top support (B1) to the wrong side of the egg top (B).

3. Position the egg top (B) over the egg sides (A) and blanket stitch around the perimeter. Leave an opening to stuff the egg before closing the top.

Blind stitch.

4. To create the filling (C), follow the directions for creating the whipped cream for the cake (see Cake Assembly in the Sweetie Pie Bakery section, Steps 6–9, page 104).

5. Use a blind stitch to attach the filling (C) to the egg top (B) to complete the deviled egg.

Condiment Bottles

MATERIALS • Makes one ketchup and one mustard bottle.

Patterns can be found on page CD52.

Material	Amount	Cut
Red felt	9″ × 12″	Cut 1 bottle side (A), 2 bottle ends (B), 1 cap side (C), 2 cap ends (D), and 1 tip (E).
Yellow felt	9″ × 12″	Cut 1 bottle side (A), 2 bottle ends (B), 1 cap side (C), 2 cap ends (D), and 1 tip (E).
Heavyweight fusible interfacing	6″ × 6″	Cut 4 bottle end supports (B1).
½″-wide foam	4″ × 4″ square	Cut 2 cap ends (D).
Embroidery floss—red, yellow		
Stuffing		

Condiment Bottle Assembly

1. Fold the red bottle side (A) in half, right sides together. Sew down the long side by machine. Turn right side out.

2. Following the manufacturer's instructions, fuse bottle end supports (B1) to the wrong sides of the red bottle ends (B).

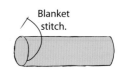

Blanket stitch.

3. Position the bottle side (A) over a bottle end (B). Using a blanket stitch, stitch around the perimeter to attach the side to the end.

4. Stuff the bottle full of stuffing. Position the other bottle end (B) over the stuffing and stitch around the perimeter with a blanket stitch. Set aside.

5. Fold the red cap side (C) in half, right sides together. Sew the short ends together by machine. Trim the seam allowance and turn right side out.

6. Position the cap side (C) over a red cap end (D) with wrong sides together, and stitch around the perimeter with a blanket stitch.

7. Insert a foam cap end (D) into the base you just created. Place the other red cap end (D) over the top and blanket stitch around the perimeter.

8. Fold the red tip (E) in half, right sides together. Sew the straight edges together by machine. Turn right side out.

9. Stuff the tip (E) and center it over the cap end (D). Use a whipstitch to attach them.

10. Place the assembled cap over the bottle. Use a blind stitch to stitch around the perimeter of the bottom of the cap to complete the ketchup bottle.

11. Repeat Steps 1–10 with the yellow felt to complete the mustard bottle.

Spatula

MATERIALS • Makes one spatula.

Patterns can be found on page CD53.

Material	Amount	Cut
Gray felt	9″ × 12″	Cut 2 spatula bases (B).
Black felt	9″ × 12″	Cut 1 spatula detail (A) and 2 handles (C).
Foamcore board	4″ × 10″	Cut 1 spatula support (B1) and 1 handle support (C1).
Glue		
Embroidery floss—gray, black		

Spatula Assembly

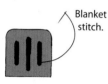

Blanket stitch.

1. Use a blanket stitch to secure the spatula detail (A) to the right side of a spatula base (B). Place the spatula bases (B) wrong sides together and use a blanket stitch to sew around the perimeter, leaving the lower edge open. Set aside.

Blanket stitch.

2. Place the 2 handles (C) wrong sides together. Use a blanket stitch to stich around the hole in the handle (C). Use a blanket stitch to stitch around the handle, leaving the lower edge open. Set aside.

3. Glue the spatula support (B1) to the handle support (C1), as shown.

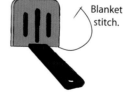

Blanket stitch.

4. Slip the handle (C) over the handle support (C1) and the spatula (B) over the spatula support (B1).

5. Use a blanket stitch to close the lower edge of the spatula (B), completing the spatula.

Baked Potato

MATERIALS • Makes one baked potato.

Patterns can be found on pages CD54 and CD55.

Material	Amount	Cut
White felt	2 sheets 9″ × 12″	Cut 2 baked potatoes (A) and 1 baked potato top (B).
Tan felt	9″ × 12″	Cut 2 baked potato skins (C).
Embroidery floss—white, tan		
Stuffing		

Baked Potato Assembly

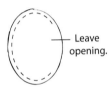

Leave opening.

1. Place 2 baked potatoes (A) right sides together. Machine sew around the perimeter, leaving an opening to turn right side out.

Blind stitch.

2. Turn the baked potato (A) right side out. Stuff. Close the opening with a blind stitch.

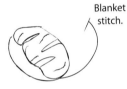

Blanket stitch.

3. Place the baked potato top (B) over the baked potato. Pin the potato top around the perimeter so it lines up with the seam of the baked potato. The top should bunch up and wrinkle. Sew around the perimeter of the top (B) with a blanket stitch to secure it to the baked potato.

Leave opening.

4. Place 2 baked potato skins (C) right sides together. Sew around the perimeter by machine, leaving an opening to turn right side out.

Blind stitch.

5. Place the baked potato with attached top inside of the potato skin (C). Blindstitch the opening closed.

6. Carefully make the slits in the top of the baked potato skin (C). First make a small slit, careful not to cut through the baked potato (A).

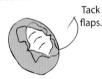

Tack flaps.

7. Fold back the openings and tack them into place with a needle and thread to complete the baked potato.

Barbecued Ribs

MATERIALS • Makes one slab of ribs.

Patterns can be found on pages CD56 and CD57.

Material	Amount	Cut
Brown felt	9″ × 12″	Cut 1 rib top (A) and 2 rib sides (B).
Ivory felt	9″ × 12″	Cut 6 rib bones (C).
Brick red felt	6″ × 6″	Cut 1 rib sauce (D).
Embroidery floss—brown, ivory, red		
Stuffing		

Barbecued Ribs Assembly

1. Fold the rib top (A) in half widthwise, right sides together. Sew the edges together by machine. Turn right side out.

2. Attach a rib side (B) to the end of the rib top (A), using a blanket stitch.

3. Stuff the ribs. Place the other rib side (B) over the stuffing. Sew around the perimeter with a blanket stitch, leaving an opening to finish stuffing the rib before closing.

4. With a needle and embroidery floss, wrap thread around a section where indicated on the pattern. Pull the floss firmly to make an indentation to segment the rib section. Secure the thread with a knot and repeat on the other section.

5. Place 2 rib bones (C) right sides together. Sew around the curved perimeter, leaving the top open. Turn right side out. Repeat to make another 2 rib bones (C).

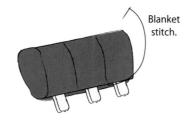

6. Stuff the rib bones. Place a rib bone (C) at the bottom of each rib section. Use a blanket stitch to secure them.

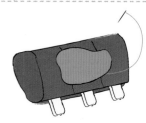

7. Place the rib sauce (D) over the ribs. Sew around the perimeter with a blanket stitch to complete the barbecued ribs.

Chef's Hat

MATERIALS • Makes one chef's hat.

Patterns can be found on pages CD58–CD72.

Material	Amount	Cut
Hat fabric	1 yard	Cut 1 circle 20″ for hat top (A) and 1 rectangle 5″ × 26″ for hat band (B).*
Lightweight fusible interfacing, such as Shape-Flex	1¼ yards (1 package)	Cut 1 rectangle 4½″ × 25½″ for hat band support (B1).
Double-fold bias tape	1 package	
Hook-and-loop tape, ⅝″ wide	1½″	

* Use the band pattern provided or adjust the length to fit your child's head as follows: The width of the band should be 5″. To find the length, measure the circumference of the child's head, and then add 1½″ for the hat band overlap and seam allowances. Adjust the length of pattern B1, hat band support, accordingly.

Chef's Hat Assembly

1. Following the manufacturer's instructions, fuse the band support (B1) to the wrong side of the band (B).

2. Fold the band (B) in half lengthwise, right sides together. Sew the short ends together. Clip corners and turn right side out. Baste the long edges together.

3. Sew a gathering stitch all around the perimeter of the hat top (A) a scant ¼″ inside the edge.

4. Adjust the gathers of the hat top (A) to fit the long edge of the band (B). *Note that the short ends of the hat band overlap each other by 1″.* Pin the hat band and the hat top right sides together and then stitch all around.

5. Cut a piece of bias tape the same length as the seam from Step 4 plus 1½″.

6. Unfold the bias tape and turn the short ends under ¼″. Refold the bias tape.

7. Encase the seam allowances from Step 4 in the bias tape, overlapping the short ends of the bias tape. Stitch all around.

8. Sew the hook-and-loop tape at the short ends of the hat band to close the hat band.

Apron

MATERIALS • Makes one apron.

Material	Amount	Cut
Main fabric	1 yard	Follow cutting instructions below.
Lining fabric	1 yard	Follow cutting instructions below.
1″ D-rings	2	

Making the Template

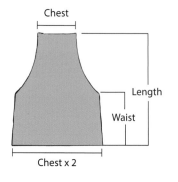

1. Measure your child's chest. Divide that measurement by 3 to get the *apron chest measurement*. The width of the bottom edge is twice the apron chest measurement.

Measure from the top of your child's chest to his/her knee to determine the *apron length measurement*.

Measure from your child's waist to his/her knee to determine the *apron waist measurement*.

2. Draft an apron template using the diagram above with your child's measurements.

3. To create a place for the arms, draw a slight curve starting at the top corner of the chest, down to the waist measurement, as shown.

From Main Fabric

Cut the apron from the main fabric using the created template.

Cut 3 strips 4″ × 25″ for the straps.

From Lining Fabric

Cut the apron from the lining fabric using the created template.

Apron Assembly

1. To create the straps, fold a strip in half lengthwise with wrong sides together and press.

2. Sew down the long edge, pivot at the corner, and sew the short end. Leave the other end open. Turn the strip right side out and press. Repeat with the other 2 strips.

— Leave open.

3. Measure 5″ from the open end of a strap and cut.

4. Insert the 5″ strap through both D-rings. Fold the strap in half, matching raw edges. Baste the ends together.

5. Pin the strap piece with the D-rings in the upper corner on the right side of the apron front. Pin the raw end of the 20″ strap in the other upper corner. Pin the raw ends of the remaining 2 straps at the waist as shown. Baste all straps in place by machine.

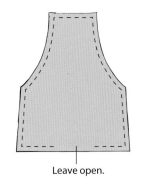

Leave open.

6. Place the lining fabric over the apron front with attached straps, right sides together.

7. Sew around the perimeter of the apron, leaving an opening in the bottom as shown. Clip the corners and turn right side out. Press the apron and make sure to press the seam allowance in at the opening.

8. Topstitch around the perimeter of the apron, securing the seam allowance of the opening, completing the apron.

To Market, to Market

One of my favorite imaginative settings as a child was the supermarket. I loved pretending I had the adult responsibilities of grocery shopping, weighing the produce, and paying the cashier. The realism of the food made it even more fun. I created each part of the market with this in mind. It was my goal to make the items look as realistic as possible with just a touch of whimsy so they would still be magical to play with.

Apple

MATERIALS • Makes one apple.

Patterns can be found on page CD73.

Material	Amount	Cut
Red felt	9″ × 12″	Cut 6 apple segments (A).
Light brown felt	3″ × 3″	Cut 1 stem (B) and 1 stem top (C).
Kelly green felt	3″ × 3″	Cut 1 small leaf (D).
Dark green felt	3″ × 3″	Cut 1 large leaf (E).
Embroidery floss—red, brown, green		
Stuffing		

Apple Assembly

1. Place 2 apple segments (A) right sides together, aligning the registration dots. Sew the curved seam by machine, stitching between dots. Repeat so you have 3 pairs.

2. Open the apple segments and place 2 pairs right sides together, aligning the dots. Sew the curved seam by machine.

3. Open the apple segments and add the final pair. Sew the curved seam by machine.

4. When sewing the final curved seam, leave an opening to turn the apple right side out.

Blind stitch.

Blanket stitch.

5. Stuff the apple and use a blind stitch to sew the seam closed. Set aside.

6. Fold the stem (B) in half, right sides together. Sew the short edge by machine.

7. Turn the stem (B) right side out. Use a blanket stitch to attach the stem top (C), right side out, over the opening in the stem (B).

8. Stuff the stem. Set aside.

Running stitch.

Whipstitch.

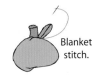
Blanket stitch.

9. Lay the small leaf (D) centered on the large leaf (E) and sew a running stitch down the center of the 2 leaves.

10. Use a whipstitch to secure the end of the leaf to the top of the apple.

11. Place the stem over the leaf and secure it with a blanket stitch to complete the apple.

Banana

MATERIALS • Makes one banana.

Patterns can be found on page CD74.

Material	Amount	Cut
Yellow felt	9″ × 12″	Cut 1 banana top (C), 2 banana sides (D), and 1 banana bottom (E).
Brown felt	3″ × 3″	Cut 1 banana stem (A) and 1 stem top (B).
Embroidery floss— yellow, brown		
Stuffing		

Banana Assembly

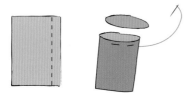

Blanket stitch.

1. Fold the banana stem (A) in half right sides together. Sew the long edge together. Trim and turn right side out. Use a blanket stitch to attach the stem top (B) to the end of the tube. Stuff the stem and set aside.

2. Using a blanket stitch, attach the banana top (C) to a banana side (D). Repeat, attaching the other banana side (D) to the top (C).

3. Use a blanket stitch to attach the banana bottom (E) to the banana sides (D). Before closing the banana bottom, stuff the banana and insert the banana stem. Secure in place with stitches.

Orange

MATERIALS • Makes one orange.

Patterns can be found on page CD75.

Material	Amount	Cut
Orange felt	9″ × 12″	Cut 6 orange segments (A).
Lime green felt	1″ × 1″	Cut 1 orange stem (B).
Embroidery floss—orange, green		
Stuffing		

Orange Assembly

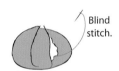

Blind stitch.

1. Place 2 orange segments (A) right sides together and registration dots aligned. Sew down a curved side, stitching between the dots.

2. Repeat, sewing the rest of the segments together in turn. Sew the final segment, leaving a 2″ opening in the middle of the arc. Turn right side out.

3. Stuff the orange and blindstitch to close the opening.

4. Place the orange stem (B) over the top of the orange where all of the points meet. Stitch it into place.

Grapes

MATERIALS • Makes one bunch of grapes.

Patterns can be found on page CD75.

Material	Amount	Cut
Light brown felt	9″ × 12″	Cut 2 (1 and 1 reversed) grape stems (B).
Purple felt	9″ × 12″	Cut 40 grapes (A).
Pipe cleaners	4	
Embroidery floss—purple, brown		
Stuffing		

Grapes Assembly

1. Twist 2 pipe cleaners together. Repeat to make 2 twisted sets.

2. Cut a twisted set of pipe cleaners into 3 pieces: 3½″, 2½″, and 6″. Twist the sets of pipe cleaners onto each other using the grape stem (B) as a template.

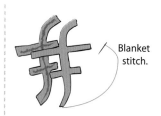

Blanket stitch.

3. Position the pipe cleaners over the wrong side of a grape stem (B). Set the other grape stem (B) on top and blanket stitch around the perimeter. Set aside.

4. Place 2 grapes (A) right sides together.

5. Sew around the perimeter by machine, leaving an opening to turn right side out.

Blind stitch.

6. Turn the grape right side out and stuff. Blindstitch the opening closed.

7. Repeat Steps 4–6 to complete 20 grapes.

Blind stitch.

8. Use a blind stitch to attach each grape to the stem.

Pineapple

MATERIALS • Makes one pineapple.

Patterns can be found on pages CD76–CD78.

Material	Amount	Cut
Yellow-orange felt, 40″ wide	⅓ yard	Cut 2 pineapple sides (A).
Dark green felt	9″ × 12″	Cut 1 large pineapple crown (B) and 1 small pineapple crown (C).
Embroidery floss—yellow, green		
Stuffing		

Pineapple Assembly

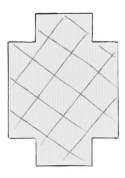

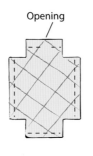

Opening

1. Use a sewing machine and brown thread to sew 45°-angle diagonal lines about 1¼″ apart on the right side of each pineapple side (A). Repeat sewing the lines in the opposite direction, crisscrossing the previous lines.

2. Place the pineapple sides (A) together, right sides facing. Sew the top, bottom, and sides together by machine, leaving a 2″ opening on the top seam for turning.

3. Open the corners on the bottom of the pineapple. Use a machine to sew the corners together. Repeat for the top corners.

4. Turn the pineapple right side out. Stuff and sew the opening closed with a blind stitch.

Roll.

Whipstitch.

5. Starting at an end, roll up the large pineapple crown (B). Secure by placing a few stitches through the bottom.

6. Wrap the small pineapple crown (C) around the large crown (B). Secure by placing a few stitches through the bottom.

7. Place the completed crown on top of the pineapple. Secure the crown to the pineapple using a whipstitch to complete the pineapple.

Carrot

MATERIALS • Makes one carrot.

Patterns can be found on pages CD79–CD81.

Material	Amount	Cut
Orange felt	9″ × 12″	Cut 2 carrot halves (A) and 1 carrot top (B).
Kelly green felt	4½″ × 18″	Cut 1 leaf (C).
Embroidery floss—orange, green		
Stuffing		

Carrot Assembly

1. Place the carrot halves (A) right sides together. Sew down a side, pivot at the tip, and sew up the other side. Turn right side out.

2. Stuff carrot.

Blanket stitch.

3. Place the carrot top (B) over the stuffing and attach it with a blanket stitch.

4. Fold the leaf (C) in half lengthwise, right sides together. Sew the long open edge by machine. Turn right side out.

5. Position the seam on the center back of the tube. On each side of the seam, make slits ¼″ apart.

Baste.

6. Sew a basting stitch down the center of the leaf with a needle and thread. Pull the thread taut and gather the leaf.

Whipstitch.

7. Take the 2 open ends and use a whipstitch to secure them to the carrot top (B).

8. With orange floss, sew long running stitches, randomly placed around the body of the carrot, to add dimension (see project photo, above).

Asparagus

MATERIALS • Makes one bundle of asparagus.

Patterns can be found on page CD82.

Material	Amount	Cut
Olive green felt	2 sheets 9″ × 12″	Cut 6 asparagus pieces (A).
Lime green felt	4″ × 4″	Cut 18 asparagus leaves (B).
Purple felt	1″ × 5″	Cut 1 band (C).
Embroidery floss—green, purple		

Asparagus Assembly

← Roll.

Whipstitch.

1. Roll up 1 asparagus (A) lengthwise and secure the side with a blanket stitch.

2. Use a whipstitch to attach 3 asparagus leaves (B) to the side of the asparagus stalk.

3. Repeat Steps 1–2 to create 5 more asparagus stalks.

4. Wrap the band (C) around the asparagus bundle and secure the ends with a needle and thread to complete the asparagus.

Eggplant

MATERIALS • Makes one eggplant.

Patterns can be found on page CD83.

Material	Amount	Cut
Purple felt	9″ × 12″	Cut 2 eggplant pieces (A).
Kelly green felt	6″ × 6″	Cut 1 eggplant leaf (B), 4 stem sides (C), and 1 stem top (D).
Embroidery floss—green		
Stuffing		

Eggplant Assembly

1. Place the 2 eggplant pieces (A) right sides together. Sew around the perimeter, leaving a 2″ opening at the bottom for turning. Clip the curves, and then turn right side out.

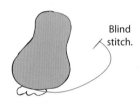

Blind stitch.

2. Stuff the eggplant and blind-stitch the opening closed.

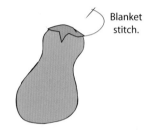

Blanket stitch.

3. Place the eggplant leaf (B) over the top of the eggplant and blanket stitch around the perimeter to secure it in place. Set aside.

Blanket stitch.

4. Place 2 eggplant stem sides (C) wrong sides together. Use a blanket stitch to sew up the angled side of the stem, attaching the 2 pieces. Repeat to attach each stem side (C) in turn, until all 4 sides are sewn together.

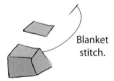

Blanket stitch.

5. Place the stem top (D) over the top of the sewn stem sides, and attach it with a blanket stitch.

Blanket stitch.

6. Stuff the stem and position it over the center of the leaf. Use a blanket stitch to sew around the perimeter of the base of the stem, attaching it to the leaf.

Potato

MATERIALS • Makes one potato.

Patterns can be found on page CD84.

Material	Amount	Cut
Light brown felt	9″ × 12″	Cut 2 (1 and 1 reversed) potatoes (A).
Embroidery floss—ecru		
Stuffing		

Potato Assembly

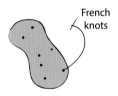

French knots

Clip curves.

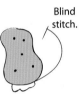

Blind stitch.

1. Sew French knots on the right side of each potato (A) half.

2. Place the potato (A) pieces right sides together and sew around the perimeter by machine, leaving a 2″ opening for turning. Clip the curves and turn right side out.

3. Stuff the potato and blind-stitch the opening closed to complete the potato.

Lettuce

MATERIALS • Makes one romaine lettuce.

Patterns can be found on pages CD85 and CD86.

Material	Amount	Cut
Lime green felt	9″ × 12″	Cut 3 small lettuce leaves (A).
Kelly green felt	9″ × 12″	Cut 3 medium lettuce leaves (B).
Dark green felt	9″ × 12″	Cut 3 large lettuce leaves (C) and 1 lettuce base (D).
Embroidery floss—dark green		

Lettuce Assembly

1. Layer the medium lettuce leaves (B) alternately with the small lettuce leaves (A), overlapping them about halfway.

2. Gently roll the overlapped leaves at the base to form a circular shape with all 6 leaves.

Make stitches.

3. Using a needle and thread, create stitches through the bottom of the leaves to secure them together.

4. Using a sewing machine, sew the vein detail onto the large lettuce leaves (C) and lettuce base (D) using white thread.

5. Layer the large lettuce leaves (C) around the rest of the lettuce leaves and pin into place. Using a needle and thread, stitch through the bottom of the leaves to secure them together.

Blanket stitch.

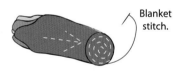

6. Use a blanket stitch to attach the lettuce base (D) to the bottom of the lettuce leaves, completing the lettuce.

Canned Goods

MATERIALS • Makes two cans.

Patterns can be found on pages CD87 and CD88.

Material	Amount	Cut
Gray felt	9″ × 12″	Cut 4 can tops (A).
Aqua felt	9″ × 12″	Cut 1 tuna label (B).
Blue felt	9″ × 12″	Cut 1 soup label (C).
Scrap fabric for accent	2″ × 2″	
Heavyweight fusible interfacing	⅛ yard	Cut 4 can top supports (A1).
Embroidery floss—light blue, yellow, gray		
Stuffing		

Canned Goods Assembly

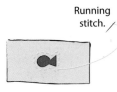

Running stitch.

1. Sew a spiral onto a can top (A) by machine. Keep moving your way around, using the presser foot as a guide, backstitching at the center. Do this for all 4 can tops (A).

2. Following the manufacturer's instructions, fuse a can top support (A1) to the wrong side of a can top (A). Repeat for all 4 can tops (A). Set aside.

3. With sharp, pointed scissors, carefully cut out the fish shape from the tuna label (B).

4. Place the accent fabric behind the fish cutout. Use a running stitch to sew around the fish, attaching the fabric.

Blanket stitch.

5. Fold the tuna label in half, with right sides together.

6. Sew the short ends together by machine. Turn right side out.

7. Position a can top (A) at the bottom of the tuna label (B). Use a blanket stitch to attach the can top to the label (B).

8. Stuff the can. Place the other can top (A) on top of the stuffing. Use a blanket stitch to sew around the perimeter. Before closing the can top (A), add enough stuffing to fill the can. Secure the thread with a knot to complete the can.

9. To create the soup can, use a split stitch to create the *S-O-U-P* letters on the soup label (C). Repeat Steps 5–8 to complete the can.

Eggs

MATERIALS • Makes one carton and six eggs.

Patterns can be found on pages CD89–CD92.

Material	Amount	Cut
White felt	3 sheets 9″ × 12″	Cut 30 egg segments (A).
Blue felt	9″ × 12″	Cut 1 logo (E).
Gray felt	½ yard	Cut 48 egg holders (B), 2 carton bases (C), 2 carton tops (D), 4 carton ends (F), 4 carton sides (G), and 1 hinge (H).
Heavyweight fusible interfacing	¼ yard	Cut 1 carton top support (D1), 2 carton end supports (F1), and 2 carton side supports (G1).
Foamcore board	8″ × 10″	Cut 1 carton base support (C1).
Embroidery floss—white, gray, teal		
Stuffing		
Glue		

Eggs Assembly

1. With right sides together, sew 2 egg segments (A) together by machine. Sew down a curved side, stitching between dots. Continue adding an egg segment (A) at a time until 5 are sewn together, leaving an opening in the last seam you sew to turn right side out.

Blind stitch.

2. Turn the egg right side out and stuff. Blindstitch the opening shut.

3. Repeat Steps 1 and 2 to make 5 more eggs.

4. Place 2 of the egg holders (B) right sides together. Sew together, by machine, along a curved side edge. Repeat with 2 more egg holders (B).

Wrong side

Right side

5. Open the 2 paired egg holder halves and place them right sides together. Sew both curved sides to attach the halves.

6. Repeat Steps 4 and 5 to make 12 egg holders.

7. Turn 6 of the egg holders right side out.

8. Place an egg holder that is wrong side out into an egg holder that is right side out, wrong sides together. Take care to align the seams. Pin the top edges together. Repeat to make 6 egg holders. Set aside.

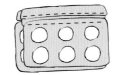

9. Following the manufacturer's directions, fuse a carton side support (G1) to the wrong side of a carton side (G). Repeat to make another interfaced carton side (G).

10. Insert the hinge (H), centered, between the egg carton bases (C) with right sides out. Stitch close to the edge of the egg carton base by machine to connect the pieces.

11. Place the other side of the hinge (H), centered, between an egg carton side (G) *with* interfacing and an egg carton side (G) *without* interfacing. Wrong sides should be facing, with the long curved edge of the side at the hinge. Sew close to the side edge by machine to connect the pieces.

12. Glue the foamcore board carton base support (C1), centered, between the carton base pieces (C), which are attached to the hinge.

13. Insert an egg holder from Step 8 into a base opening. Sew around the perimeter of the opening with a blanket stitch to attach the holder to all layers of the base. Repeat with the rest of the egg holders. Set aside.

Blanket stitch.

14. Use a running stitch to attach the egg logo (E) letters to a carton top (D).

Running stitch.

E66S

15. Fuse the carton top support (D1), centered, to the wrong side of the other carton top (D).

16. Fuse a carton end support (F1), centered, to the wrong side of a carton end (F). Repeat to make another interfaced carton end.

17. Pin an interfaced carton end (F) to a carton end (F) without interfacing, wrong sides facing. Repeat to pin another carton end (F), the remaining carton side (G) pieces, and the carton top (D) pieces.

18. Beginning with the carton side with attached hinge, connect the sides to the carton top (D) through all layers with a blanket stitch. When you reach a corner, add an end piece (F), and continue until all 4 sides are attached to the top.

19. Connect each corner with a blanket stitch, a corner at a time.

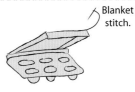

Blanket stitch.

20. Sew around the perimeter of the lid and the base to complete the egg carton.

Cereal

MATERIALS • Makes one box of cereal.

Patterns can be found on pages CD93 and CD94.

Material	Amount	Cut
Red-orange felt	3 sheets 9″ × 12″	Cut 2 box fronts (A), 2 box tops (B), and 2 box sides (C).
White felt	9″ × 12″	Cut 1 box logo (D).
Yellow-orange felt	3″ × 6″	Cut 2 fruityO pieces (E).
Lime green felt	3″ × 6″	Cut 2 fruityO pieces (E).
Orange felt	3″ × 3″	Cut 1 fruityO piece (E).
Aqua felt	3″ × 6″	Cut 2 fruityO pieces (E).
Green felt	3″ × 3″	Cut 1 fruityO piece (E).
Purple felt	3″ × 6″	Cut 2 fruityO pieces (E).
2″-thick foam	7″ × 9″	Cut 1 box front (A).
Embroidery floss—purple, red, yellow, green, orange, blue		

Cereal Box Assembly

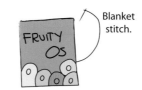

1. Use a running stitch to attach the box logo (D) to a box front (A).

2. Arrange the fruityO pieces (E) on the box front (A) and attach with a blanket stitch.

3. Place the box front (A) and a box top (B) in their corresponding places over the foam. Use a blanket stitch to attach the pieces.

4. When you reach the corner, add a box side (C), and continue working your way around the foam, attaching the box tops (B) and sides (C) to the box front (A).

5. When each of the 4 sides is attached, stitch each corner in turn with a blanket stitch.

6. Place the remaining box front (A) over the foam and use a blanket stitch to attach it, completing the cereal box.

Grocery Bag

MATERIALS • Makes one grocery bag.

Pattern can be found on page CD95.

Material	Amount	Cut
Light brown felt, 36″ wide	½ yard	Cut 2 rectangles 15″ × 15¾″ for bag (no pattern provided).
Green felt	9″ × 12″	Cut 1 market logo.
Embroidery floss—green		

Grocery Bag Assembly

1. Trim the 15″ top edge of each bag rectangle with pinking shears or a pinking blade on a rotary cutter. Cut 3″ × 3″ squares from each bottom corner.

2. Use a blanket stitch to attach each piece of the market logo to a bag piece.

3. Position the 2 bag pieces right sides together. Sew down each side and across the bottom of the bag.

4. Open up the bottom corner of the bag and align the seams, right sides together. Pin and stitch across the corner. Repeat on the other side.

5. Turn the bag right side out. Fold a side together from the corner to the top edge, wrong sides together. Topstitch ⅛″ from the fold to make a narrow pleat. Repeat, a side at a time, to complete the grocery bag.

Money

MATERIALS • Makes three dollars.

Patterns can be found on page CD96.

Material	Amount	Cut
Olive green felt	9″ × 12″	Cut 6 dollars (A).
Freezer paper	3″ × 6″	Cut 1 freezer-paper stencil using dollar silhouette (B).
Gold metallic fabric paint		
Embroidery floss—green, gold		

Dollar Assembly

1. Use the freezer-paper stencil and gold metallic paint to stencil the dollar silhouette (B) onto 3 dollars (A). Refer to Freezer-Paper Stenciling (page 139). Set aside to dry.

2. Cut the oval from the other 3 dollars (A).

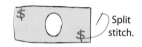

Split stitch.

3. Sew a dollar symbol using a split stitch in 2 corners of each dollar with the cutout.

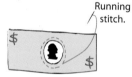

Running stitch.

4. Once the silhouette is dry, position it behind a dollar with the cutout and sew a running stitch around the center oval to secure the 2 layers.

Blanket stitch.

5. Stitch the outside edges with a blanket stitch to complete the dollars.

Bread

MATERIALS

Makes one loaf of bread and bag.

Patterns can be found on pages CD97–CD102.

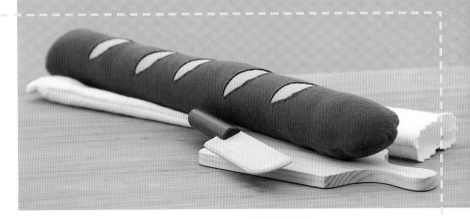

Material	Amount	Cut
Brown felt, 36″ wide	¼ yard	Cut 1 bread base (A) and 1 bread top (B).
Tan felt	6″ × 6″	Cut 5 bread insets (C).
White felt, 36″ wide	⅓ yard	Cut 2 bread bags (D).
Heavyweight fusible interfacing	¼ yard	Cut 1 bread base support (A1).
Embroidery floss—tan, light brown		
Stuffing		

Bread Assembly

1. Following the manu-facturer's instructions, fuse the bread base support (A1), centered, to the wrong side of the bread base (A).

2. With sharp scissors, cut the 5 openings from the bread top (B).

3. Position the bread insets (C) behind the openings in the bread top (B). Use a sewing machine to sew a narrow seam around the perimeter of each opening, attaching the bread top (B) to the bread insets (C). Trim away excess inset fabric.

4. Place the bread base and bread top right sides together. Sew around the perimeter by machine, leaving an opening to turn right side out.

Blind stitch.

5. Turn the bread right side out and stuff. Use a blind stitch to close the opening. Set aside.

6. Trim a short end of each bread bag (D) piece with pinking shears or a pinking blade on a rotary cutter.

7. Place the bag (D) pieces right sides together. Sew around the sides and bottom by machine.

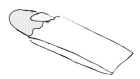

8. Turn the bag right side out and slide the bread inside.

Milk

MATERIALS • Makes one carton of milk.

Patterns can be found on pages CD103 and CD104.

Material	Amount	Cut
White felt	2 sheets 9″ × 12″	Cut 4 milk sides (A), 1 milk bottom (C), 2 milk top ends (D), 2 milk top sides (E), and 2 milk tops (F).
Blue felt	9″ × 12″	Cut 1 milk logo (B).
fast2fuse heavy double-sided stiff fusible interfacing	1″ × 4½″	Cut 1 milk top support (F1).
2″-thick foam	10″ × 10″	Cut 2 milk top ends (D) and 2 milk sides (A).

Milk Assembly

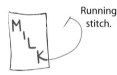

Running stitch.

1. Position the milk logo (B) in place on a milk side (A). Use a running stitch to attach the logo to the side.

Blanket stitch.

2. Place the 2 foam milk sides (A) together and pin the corresponding felt milk sides (A) and milk bottom (C) in place.

3. Use a blanket stitch to attach each milk side to the milk bottom (C). Work your way around all 4 sides of the base.

4. Use a blanket stitch to stitch up each corner edge in turn. Set aside.

5. To add the top, place the 2 foam milk top ends (D) together and pin the corresponding felt milk top sides (E) and felt milk top ends (D) in place.

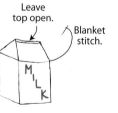

Leave top open.

Blanket stitch.

6. Place the assembled top from Step 5 on the assembled milk carton from Step 4. Starting with the milk top side (E), use a blanket stitch to attach the side to the top. Work your way around all 4 sides of the top.

7. Use a blanket stitch to stitch up each corner edge of the top in turn. Do not close the top, pointed edge of the milk carton.

8. Following the manufacturer's instructions, fuse the milk top support (F1) to the wrong side of a milk top (F). Pin the milk top (F) with interfacing to the milk top (F) without interfacing, wrong sides together.

Running stitch.

9. Insert the milk top into the opening in the top, pointed edge of the milk carton. Use a running stitch to attach the milk top to the top point. After you've attached it, stitch around the perimeter of the milk top with a blanket stitch to complete the milk carton.

Butter

MATERIALS • Makes one box of butter.

Patterns can be found on page CD105.

Material	Amount	Cut
Blue felt	9″ × 12″	Cut 1 butter logo (B).
Yellow-orange felt	9″ × 12″	Cut 4 butter sides (A) and 2 butter ends (C).
2″-thick foam	3″ × 5″	Cut 1 butter side (A).
1″-thick foam	3″ × 5″	Cut 1 butter side (A).
Embroidery floss—blue, yellow		

Butter Assembly

Blanket stitch.

1. Use a blanket stitch to attach the butter logo (B) to a butter side (A).

2. Stack the 2 foam pieces so that the stack measures 3″ × 3″ × 5″. Pin a felt butter side (A) to each side of the foam stack.

Blanket stitch.

3. Use a blanket stitch to sew across the bottom of 2 butter sides (A) to connect them. When you reach the corner, sew the next butter side (A). Continue until each side has been attached.

4. Place a butter end (C) over an end and use a blanket stitch to stitch around the perimeter to join the end to the sides. Repeat with the other butter end to complete the butter.

Crackers

MATERIALS • Makes one cracker box.

Patterns can be found on pages CD106 and CD107.

Material	Amount	Cut
Aqua felt	2 sheets 9″ × 12″	Cut 2 cracker box fronts (A), 2 cracker box sides (C), and 2 cracker box ends (D).
Orange felt	9″ × 12″	Cut 1 cracker box logo (B).
2″-thick foam	6″ × 9″	Cut 1 cracker box front (A).
Embroidery floss— blue, orange		

Cracker Box Assembly

Running stitch.

1. Use a running stitch to attach the cracker box logo (B) to a cracker box front (A).

2. Place the cracker box front (A) with attached appliqué logo and a cracker box side (C) in place over the foam. Join the front and side pieces using a blanket stitch.

Blanket stitch.

3. Add the next cracker box front (A) to the cracker box side (C) and so on until all of the sides have been attached.

4. Place the cracker box end (D) over the foam and sew around the perimeter with a blanket stitch. Repeat with the other cracker box end (D) to complete the cracker box.

Pasta

MATERIALS • Makes one bag of pasta.

Patterns can be found on pages CD108 and CD109.

Material	Amount	Cut
Tan felt	9″ × 12″	Cut 20 noodles (A).
White felt	2 sheets 9″ × 12″	Cut 2 pasta bags (B).
Red felt	4″ × 6″	Cut 1 pasta logo (D).
Medium-weight clear vinyl, such as Quilter's Vinyl	6″ × 6″	Cut 1 pasta window (C).
White hook-and-loop tape	1″ × 2½″	
Embroidery floss		

Pasta Assembly

1. Trim the short sides of a noodle (A) with pinking shears or a pinking blade.

2. Run a basting stitch through the center of a noodle (A). Pull thread to gather and tie a knot to secure.

3. Repeat Steps 1 and 2 to create 20 noodles.

4. Use sharp scissors to cut the circle from a pasta bag (B) piece.

5. Use a running stitch to attach the pasta logo (D) to the pasta bag (B) with circle removed.

6. Place the clear pasta window (C) behind the circle cutout on the pasta bag (B) with logo. Sew ⅛″ around the outside of the window by machine.

7. Place the pasta bag (B) with logo and the pasta bag (B) without logo right sides together. Sew down each side and across the bottom.

8. Open the bottom corners and align the seams. Sew each corner together. Turn the bag right side out.

Hook tape.

9. Use the sewing machine to sew the hook side of the hook-and-loop tape to the center of the top edge of the pasta bag (B) without a logo. No need to attach the loop side of the tape; the hooks on the tape will attach to the felt.

10. Insert the pasta and roll the top of the bag closed to complete.

Sweetie Pie Bakery

When I began designing sewing patterns, my first line was called Sweetie Pie Bakery. At the time that my daughter was born, we were running our family restaurant, where I did all of the baking. For my little girl, I wanted to fashion a magical world of pastries, full of pink and sparkle, so she could create her own treats right alongside me. I designed this pattern with a hinged bakery box so that little ones could enjoy taking the treats in and out. Older children can interact by playing bakery and serving up fresh baked goods.

Scone

A great project for little hands is to help with the embellishments. I find it helpful to hand my daughter a bag of buttons and talk about them as I'm sewing. We count, sort colors, and create patterns as I work, and she picks out the finishing touches!

MATERIALS • Makes one scone.

Patterns can be found on page CD110.

Material	Amount	Cut
Tan felt	9″ × 12″	Cut 2 scone bases (A) and 1 scone side (B).
1″-thick foam	5″ × 5″	Cut 1 scone base (A).
Small decorative buttons for embellishments	5	
Embroidery floss—tan		
Stuffing	Small handful	

Scone Assembly

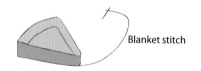

Blanket stitch

1. Fold the scone side (B) in half crosswise, with right sides together. Using a sewing machine, sew the short ends together. Turn right side out.

2. Place the scone side (B) around a scone base (A) with wrong sides together. Use a blanket stitch to stitch around the perimeter, attaching the side to the base.

3. Insert the foam scone base (A) inside the unit from Step 2.

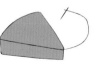

4. Place the other scone base (A) on top of the foam, with the right side up. Stitch around the perimeter of the top of the scone with a blanket stitch to attach it to the side. Stop sewing a few inches before the end and add stuffing to round out the top of the scone so it has a slightly puffy appearance as if it were fresh from the oven.

5. After you've sewn the opening shut, it is time to decorate the scone. Sew on the embellishments your little one has chosen, or if your child is a bit older, allow him or her to sew. Buttons are a great project for beginning sewers!

Sugar Cookie

Allow little ones to choose colors and decorations for the sugar cookie. My kids get a kick out of seeing things they have imagined be created. Another fun activity is to draw some hearts on a sheet of paper and have your child color some cookies beside you as you sew.

MATERIALS • Makes one cookie.

Patterns can be found on page CD111.

Material	Amount	Cut
Ivory felt	9″ × 12″	Cut 2 sugar cookie bases (B) and 1 sugar cookie side (C).
Teal felt	4″ × 4″	Cut 1 sugar cookie icing (A).
½″-thick foam	4½″ × 4½″	Cut 1 sugar cookie base (B).
Embroidery floss—ivory, pink		

Sugar Cookie Assembly

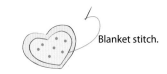

French knots

1. Sew French knots onto the sugar cookie icing (A) with pink embroidery floss.

Blanket stitch.

2. Place the sugar cookie icing (A) over the top of a sugar cookie base (B) with right sides facing up. Stitch around the perimeter of the sugar cookie icing (A) with pink embroidery floss using a blanket stitch. Set aside.

3. Fold the sugar cookie side (C) in half crosswise, with right sides together. Sew the short ends together by machine. Turn right side out.

Blanket stitch.

4. Place the sugar cookie side (C) around the plain sugar cookie base (B) with wrong sides together. Using a blanket stitch, stitch around the perimeter, attaching the side to the base.

5. Insert the foam sugar cookie base inside of the cookie.

Blanket stitch.

6. Place the sugar cookie base (B) with attached icing on top of the foam, with right side up. Stitch around the perimeter of the top of the sugar cookie with a blanket stitch to complete the sugar cookie.

Lemon Curd Tart

MATERIALS • Makes one lemon curd tart with blueberries.

Patterns can be found on page CD112.

Material	Amount	Cut
Pale yellow felt	9″ × 12″	Cut 1 lemon curd side (A) and 2 lemon curd bases (B).
Tan felt	9″ × 12″	Cut 2 tart crusts (C).
Blue felt	9″ × 12″	Cut 3 blueberries (D).
White felt	2″ × 2″	Cut 3 blueberry details (E).
½″-thick foam	4½″ × 4½″	Cut 1 lemon curd base (B).
Embroidery floss— tan, pale yellow, blue		
Stuffing	Small handful	

Lemon Curd Tart Assembly

1. Fold the lemon curd side (A) in half crosswise, with right sides together. Sew the short ends together by machine. Turn right side out.

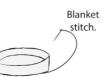

Blanket stitch.

2. Place the lemon curd side (A) around a lemon curd base (B) with wrong sides together. Use a blanket stitch to stitch around the perimeter, attaching the side to the base.

3. Insert the foam lemon curd base (B) into the unit from Step 2.

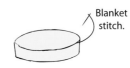

Blanket stitch.

4. Place the other felt lemon curd base (B) on top of the foam, with right sides up. Stitch around the perimeter of the top of the lemon curd with a blanket stitch to complete the lemon curd. Set aside.

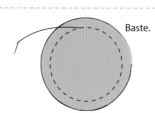

Baste.

5. Layer the 2 pieces of the tart crust (C) with wrong sides together. Baste around the perimeter on the marked lines.

6. Set the lemon curd from Step 4 inside of the basting lines of the tart crust and gently pull the basting thread to tighten up the tart crust (C). When the thread is pulled just taut enough to be firm but not buckle the lemon curd, tie a knot in the basting threads on the inside of the crust to secure them. Set aside.

Snip on line.

Baste.

7. Fold a blueberry (D) in half and make a tiny snip with scissors on a marked line. Open the blueberry (D) and fold it in half in the opposite direction. Make another small snip on the other marked line.

8. Open the blueberry (D). With wrong sides facing up, carefully glue the blueberry detail (E) over the snips you made in Step 7. Take care not to put glue where the snips were made.

9. With the wrong side of the blueberry (D) still up, run a basting stitch around the perimeter. As you pull the thread taut, begin to add stuffing to fill the blueberry.

Blind stitch.

10. Once the blueberry is stuffed full, pull the threads taut and secure them with a knot. You may need to take a few passes through the gathered section to secure the blueberry (D) closed.

11. Repeat Steps 7–10 to make 2 more blueberries.

12. Use a blind stitch to secure the blueberries to the center of the lemon curd to complete the tart.

Cupcake

MATERIALS • Makes one cupcake.

Patterns can be found on pages CD113 and CD114.

Material	Amount	Cut
Ivory felt	9″ × 12″	Cut 1 cupcake base (A), 1 cupcake side (B), and 1 cupcake top (C).
White felt	9″ × 12″	Cut 10 cupcake frosting (D).
Dark pink felt	3″ × 3″	Cut 1 cupcake gumball (E).
Light pink felt	2½″ × 2½″	Cut 1 cupcake wrapper base (G).
Cupcake wrapper fabric	8″ × 8″	Cut 1 cupcake wrapper side (F).
Heavyweight fusible interfacing	4″ × 7″	Cut 1 cupcake base support (A1) and 1 cupcake side support (B1).
Lightweight fusible interfacing, such as Shape-Flex	4″ × 7″	Cut 1 wrapper side support (F1) and 1 wrapper bottom support (G1).
Embroidery floss—ivory, pink, white		
Stuffing		

Cupcake Assembly

1. Following the manufacturer's directions, fuse the *heavyweight* interfacing (A1 and B1) to the wrong side of the cupcake base (A) and cupcake side (B).

2. Fold the cupcake side (B) in half crosswise, with right sides together. Sew the short ends together using a sewing machine. Turn right side out.

Blanket stitch.

3. Place the cupcake side (B) around the cupcake base (A) with wrong sides together. Use a blanket stitch to stitch around the perimeter and attach the pieces.

Blanket stitch.

4. Place the cupcake top (C) over the top of the cupcake side (B) and stitch around the edge with a blanket stitch to attach. Before you close the opening, fill the cupcake with stuffing. Once it is full, finish the remaining blanket stitches, securing the cupcake shut.

Frosting Assembly

Sew bottom.

Whipstitch.

1. Fold a cupcake frosting (D) in half with wrong sides together. At the fold, pinch the sides in toward the center to match the diagram. Make a few stitches in the bottom of the frosting (D) piece with a needle and thread to scrunch up the piece, and secure the thread with a knot.

2. Repeat Step 1 to create 10 frosting (D) pieces. (You may need more or fewer, depending on the placement on the cupcake top.)

3. Position each of the frosting pieces on top of the cupcake and secure each with a few whipstitches.

Gumball Assembly

Blind stitch.

1. With the wrong side of the gumball (E) facing up, run a basting stitch around the perimeter, about 3/16" in from the edge. As you pull the thread taut, begin to add the stuffing to fill the gumball.

2. Once the gumball is stuffed full, pull the threads taut and secure them with a knot. You may need to take a few passes with a needle and thread through the gathered section to secure the gumball closed.

3. Position the gumball on top of the frosting and attach it by sewing a few blind stitches until you feel that it is secure.

Cupcake Wrapper Assembly

Press pleats.

1. Fold and press pleats onto the cupcake wrapper side (F). Use the cupcake side pattern (B) as a guide to adjust the number and size of the pleats.

2. Following the manufacturer's instructions, fuse the *lightweight* interfacing (F1) to the wrong side of the pleated cupcake wrapper side (F).

3. Fold the cupcake wrapper side (F) in half crosswise, right sides together. Sew the short ends together by machine.

Blanket stitch.

4. Fuse the wrapper bottom support (G1) to the wrapper base (G). Place the wrapper base (G) on the bottom of the wrapper side (F) with wrong sides together. Stitch around the lower edge of the wrapper with a blanket stitch, attaching the base to the side.

5. Place the cupcake inside of the wrapper to complete the cupcake.

Muffin

Some people say that muffins are simply cupcakes for the breakfast table. If your little one is serving guests in the morning, an appropriate treat will need to be served! The muffin is an adaptation of the cupcake pattern—it uses cute buttons for blueberries. You could use brown buttons for chocolate chips, or red for cranberries. Let your child pick out the buttons to make any flavor imaginable!

MATERIALS • Makes one muffin.

Patterns can be found on page CD113 and CD114. This project uses the patterns for the cupcake.

Material	Amount	Cut
Tan felt	9″ × 12″	Cut 1 cupcake base (A), 1 cupcake side (B), and 1 cupcake top (C).
White felt	3″ × 3″	Cut 1 cupcake wrapper base (G).
Muffin wrapper fabric	8″ × 8″	Cut 1 cupcake wrapper side (F).
Heavyweight fusible interfacing	4″ × 7″	Cut 1 cupcake base support (A1) and 1 cupcake side support (B1).
Lightweight fusible interfacing, such as Shape-Flex	4″ × 7″	Cut 1 wrapper side support (F1) and 1 wrapper bottom support (G1).
½″ buttons for embellishments	3	
Embroidery floss—tan, white		
Stuffing		

Muffin Assembly

Follow the assembly instructions given for the cupcake project (page 100), swapping the frosting for a few simple buttons.

Cake

MATERIALS • Makes one slice of cake.

Patterns can be found on pages CD115 and CD116.

Material	Amount	Cut
Pink felt	9″ × 12″	Cut 1 cake back (B) and 1 cake base (E).
Ivory felt	9″ × 12″	Cut 1 cake side (D) and 1 cake base (E).
White felt	9″ × 12″	Cut 1 cake whipped cream (F) and 1 cake icing strip (C).
Pale yellow felt	3″ × 3″	Cut 1 cake whipped cream (F).
Mint green felt	3″ × 3″	Cut 1 cake whipped cream (F).
Dark pink felt	5″ × 5″	Cut 1 back scallop (A).
4″-thick foam (or cut 2 pieces from 2″-thick foam)	6″ × 6″	Cut 1 cake base (E).*
Embroidery floss—white, ivory, pink		

* After cutting, the foam shape looks like a 3-dimensional wedge of cake, 4″ high.

Cake Assembly

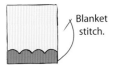

Blanket stitch.

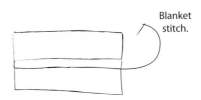

Blanket stitch.

1. Use a blanket stitch to attach the back scallop (A) to the cake back (B). Set aside.

2. Lay the cake icing (C) over the cake side (D) and pin into place. Using a blanket stitch, stitch along the top and bottom of the strip, attaching it to the cake side (D).

> **tip** When working with such a large piece of foam, I find it helpful to pin the felt pieces to the corresponding foam sides before sewing the felt pieces together.
>
> See Foam (page 10) for tips on cutting foam to size.

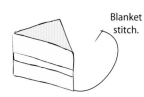

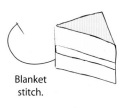

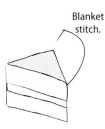

3. Beginning on the bottom, use a blanket stitch to attach the ivory cake base (E) to the pink cake back (B). Work your way around the bottom of the cake slice, stitching the ivory cake side (D) to the ivory cake base (E) next.

4. Start at the bottom corner of the cake and stitch up each of the corners in turn, attaching the ivory cake side (D) to the pink cake back (B).

5. Finally, use a blanket stitch to sew around the top perimeter of the pink cake base (E), attaching the base to the back (B) and side (D). Set aside.

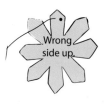

6. To make a whipped cream dollop, prepare a needle with 2 strands of floss and a knot at the base of the thread.

7. With the whipped cream (F) *wrong side up*, take the needle down and up through a felt tip just to catch the thread. Pull the thread all the way through to catch the knot.

8. Moving counterclockwise, take the needle through the next felt tip, going in from the right side and out through the wrong side. Continue this process all the way around the whipped cream (F).

9. Pull the thread taut, gathering the whipped cream (F) into a neat little dollop. Secure the thread with a knot to complete the whipped cream.

10. Following Steps 6–9, make 2 more whipped cream dollops and attach all 3 to the top of the cake with a blind stitch.

Coconut Cream Pie

While I am working on the pie slice, I let my daughter add detail to the coconut flakes. Markers work well on felt because they have a soft touch and are very similar to painting (I prefer Copic markers). Just have the little one draw on a scrap of white felt and a scrap of ivory felt to create a toasted effect. You'll be surprised how realistic it looks once you've cut it out!

MATERIALS • Makes one slice of pie.

Patterns can be found on pages CD117 and CD118.

Material	Amount	Cut
Tan felt	9″ × 12″	Cut 1 crust bottom (A), 1 pie base for crust top (D), 2 (1 and 1 reversed) crust sides (B), 1 crust front (E), 1 crust back (C), and 1 crust edge (F).
Ivory felt	9″ × 12″	Cut 2 (1 and 1 reversed) pie filling sides (G), 2 pie bases (D), and 1 pie filling back (J).
White felt	9″ × 12″	Cut 2 (1 and 1 reversed) meringue sides (I), 1 pie base for meringue bottom (D), and 1 meringue top (K).
½″-thick foam	6″ × 6″	Cut 1 crust back (C) and 1 pie base (D).
1″-thick foam	6″ × 6″	Cut 1 pie base (D) and 1 meringue top (K). *Note:* Lay the pie filling side (G) over the side of the foam filling base to create the correct side angle. Do the same with the meringue side (I) to create the correct side angle on the foam meringue top.
Embroidery floss—tan, white, ivory		

Crust and Filling Assembly

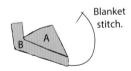

Blanket stitch.

Blanket stitch.

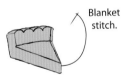

Blanket stitch.

1. Using a blanket stitch, attach the crust bottom (A) to a crust side (B). Repeat on the other side of the crust bottom (A) with the other crust side (B) piece.

2. Place the crust back (C) at the back edge of the crust unit from Step 1. Stitch the bottom seam with a blanket stitch.

3. Blanket stitch the front tip of the crust sides (B). Set aside.

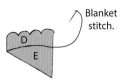

Blanket stitch.

4. Place the crust top (D) and the crust front (E) *right sides together* and blanket stitch the back edges together.

5. Set the ½˝-thick *foam* crust back (C) and crust top (D) pieces into the unit from Step 3 and position the assembled felt crust top (D) and crust front (E) from Step 4 in place.

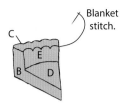

Blanket stitch.

6. Using a blanket stitch, stitch up the back side of the crust, joining the crust back (C) to a crust side (B). Next, stitch down the edge of the crust front (E) and crust top (D), attaching them to the same crust side (B).

7. Repeat Step 6 on the opposite side of the crust.

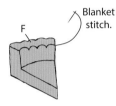

Blanket stitch.

8. To finish the crust, join the crust edge (F) to the rippled tops of the crust front and back pieces (C) and (E).

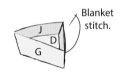

Blanket stitch.

9. Blanket stitch around the bottom perimeter of the filling, attaching the filling sides (G) to the filling bottom (D) and filling back (J).

Blanket stitch.

10. Use a blanket stitch to stitch up each of the sides in turn, attaching the filling back (J) to the filling sides (G).

11. Use a blanket stitch to stitch up the front point of the filling sides (G).

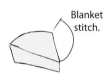

Blanket stitch.

12. Insert the 1˝-thick foam pie base (D) into the base of the filling and place the felt filling top (D) over the foam. Blanket stitch around the perimeter to secure it.

Meringue Assembly

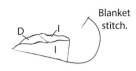

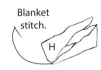

1. Blanket stitch around the bottom perimeter of the meringue base (D), attaching the meringue sides (I). Use a blanket stitch to sew up the front tip of the meringue sides.

2. Attach the base of the meringue top (H) to the back of the meringue base (D). Insert the foam meringue top (H) then stitch the felt top (H) to the sides (I), using a blanket stitch.

3. Have your little one draw on white and ivory felt scraps with a marker. I used various shades of tan and light brown marker and just let her color on the felt. You are looking for a scribble effect, as you want to see the felt through the marker, not an entirely covered sheet of felt.

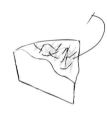

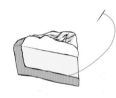

4. Cut small strips of the felt that your little one has drawn on. I suggest cutting them approximately 1/8″ × 1″.

5. Using a needle and thread, tack down the toasted coconut your little one helped you create to the top of the meringue from Step 2.

6. Use a blind stitch to connect all of the layers to complete the pie.

Bakery Box

There is a bit of magic in the moment when you open up a box of pastries to reveal what is inside. I created this box so little ones could have a peek at the delicious treats and carry them around wherever their tea parties may take them!

While I am working on the box, my daughter loves to sort through my scrap fabrics to find pieces the perfect size for the appliqués. She loves having a hand in the creation of the box.

MATERIALS • Makes one box.

Patterns can be found on pages CD119–CD130.

Material	Amount	Cut
White felt	½ yard	Cut 8 bakery box ends (A), 6 bakery box sides (B), 2 bakery box bottoms (C), 1 bakery box hinge (D), and 2 bakery box tops (E).
Fabric scraps	6 scraps 3″ × 3″	Cut 6 rectangles 2″ × 2½″ from various fabrics.
Foamcore board	1 sheet 20″ × 28″	Cut 2 bakery box end supports (A1), 2 bakery box side supports (B1), and 1 bakery box bottom support (C1).
fast2fuse heavy double-sided stiff fusible interfacing	15″ × 17″	Cut 2 bakery box end supports (A1), 2 bakery box side supports (B1), and 1 bakery box top support (E1).
Heavyweight clear vinyl, such as Quilter's Vinyl	6″ × 11″	Cut 1 bakery box window (F).
Embroidery floss—white, any color to accent fabric scraps		

Bakery Box Assembly

1. For the front of the bakery box, trace the B-A-K-E-R-Y letters (pattern G) *on the right side* of a felt bakery box side (B). Cut out the letter shapes and discard.

Running stitch.

2. Place a scrap of fabric behind each letter. With a needle and embroidery floss (I used 6 strands), stitch around the perimeter of each letter with a running stitch to secure the fabric scraps to the wrong side of the felt, creating a reverse appliqué. Set aside.

3. Following the manufacturer's directions, center and fuse a bakery box top support (E1) to the wrong side of a bakery box top (E). Place the fused box top (E) wrong sides together with the remaining box top (E).

4. Slide the vinyl window (F) between the box top pieces, centering the vinyl over the opening.

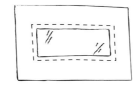

5. Using a sewing machine, topstitch around the perimeter of the window (F) to secure the vinyl.

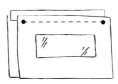

6. Place about ¼″–⅜″ of the long side of the hinge (D) inside a long end of the bakery box top unit and topstitch by machine to secure the hinge edge. Fuse together all the layers.

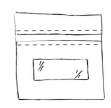

7. Using glue, center and secure the foamcore board (C1) between the felt layers of the box bottom (C) with right sides facing out. Similarly, add the foamcore boards (A1 and B1) between the felt layers for the ends (A) and sides (B). Do not glue the top long edge of one set of the box sides (B).

8. Place the unsewn long side of the hinge (D) between 2 of the bakery box sides (B), along the unglued top edge. Stitch ⅛″ from the edges to secure the hinge. Set aside.

9. Create the side and 2 ends for the top portion of the box using double-sided fusible interfacing in the same manner as the foamcore board in Step 7. Follow manufacturer's directions to fuse the interfacing in place.

10. Beginning with the bakery box bottom (C), blanket stitch down a long edge to join it with a bakery box side (B), using pieces with foamcore board from Step 7.

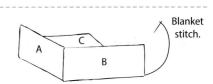

Blanket stitch.

11. Continue working your way around the perimeter of the base, attaching the bakery box bottom (C) to all sides (B) and ends (A), using pieces with foamcore board from Step 7.

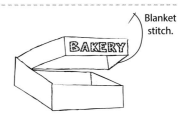

Blanket stitch.

12. Once the bottom has been attached to the sides, stitch up each corner edge with a blanket stitch, a corner at a time.

13. Stitch around the top edge of the sides to finish the bottom of the bakery box.

14. Assemble the top in the same way that you constructed the bottom, following Steps 10–13, completing the bakery box.

Tiered Cake Stand

MATERIALS • Makes one large and one small cake stand.

Patterns can be found on pages CD131–CD142.

Material	Amount	Cut
White felt	1 yard	Cut 2 large plate scallops (A), 2 large plates (B), 1 large stand base (C), 1 large stand bottom (D), 1 large stand top (E), 2 small plate scallops (F), 2 small plates (G), 1 small stand base (H), 1 small stand bottom (I), and 1 small stand top (J).
Heavyweight fusible interfacing	¼ yard	Cut 1 large plate scallop support (A1), 1 large stand base support (C1), 1 small plate scallop support (F1), and 1 small stand base support (H1).
Foamcore board	1 sheet 20″ × 28″	Cut 1 large plate support (B1), 1 large stand bottom support (D1), 1 large stand top support (E1), 1 small plate support (G1), 1 small stand bottom support (I1), and 1 small stand top support (J1).
Hot glue gun		
White rice	1½ cups	
Embroidery floss—white		

Large Cake Stand Plate Assembly

1. Fold a large plate scallop (A) in half, right sides together. Sew the short ends together by machine. Turn right side out. Set aside.

2. With the other large plate scallop (A), following manufacturer's directions, fuse the heavyweight interfacing large plate scallop support (A1) to the wrong side.

3. Fold the large plate scallop (A) with attached interfacing right sides together, and sew the short ends together with a sewing machine.

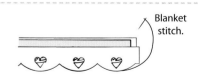

Blanket stitch.

4. Slip the large plate scallop (A) with attached interfacing inside of the large plate scallop (A), wrong sides together.

5. Use a blanket stitch to stitch around the perimeter of each heart.

6. Beginning at the seam, use a blanket stitch to sew along the bottom perimeter of the scallops. Set aside.

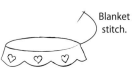

Blanket stitch.

7. Center and glue the large foamcore board plate support (B1) between 2 large plates (B) with right sides facing out.

8. Position the large plate scallop (A) around the large plate with attached support (B and B1), and blanket stitch around the perimeter to connect the pieces. Set aside.

Large Cake Stand Base Assembly

1. Fuse the large stand base support (C1) to the wrong side of the large stand base (C).

2. Fold the large stand base (C), with attached interfacing, right sides together. Sew down the straight edge by machine. Turn right side out.

3. Glue the large stand bottom support (D1) to the large stand bottom (D). Repeat with the large stand top and its support (E and E1).

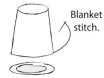

Blanket stitch.

Blanket stitch.

4. Use a blanket stitch to attach the large stand bottom (D) to the large stand base (C) you previously sewed in Step 2.

5. Fill the base nearly full of white rice. This will give the base some weight since the felt is so light.

6. Attach the large stand top from Step 3 to the base with a blanket stitch.

7. With a generous amount of hot glue, secure the assembled base to the bottom of the cake plate you set aside in Large Cake Stand Plate Assembly, Step 8.

Small Cake Stand Assembly

1. Repeat Large Cake Stand Plate Assembly, Steps 1–8 (pages 110–111) using the small plate templates.

2. Repeat Large Cake Stand Base Assembly, Steps 1–7 (above) using the small base templates.

3. With a generous amount of hot glue, secure the small cake plate to the center of the top of the large cake plate to complete the tiered cake stand.

Outdoor Explorer

All children fancy a backyard tree house, but what they really long for is a space of their own to create daydreams and discover the world around them, on their own terms. I created this fun tepee for both of my children to enjoy the outdoors together. The felt on the bottom, representing grass, allows them to decorate the exterior themselves with bugs and butterflies, camouflaging their play space.

MATERIALS • Makes one tepee, five insects, and one comfy quilt.

Patterns can be found on pages CD143–CD204.

Material	Amount	Cut
Duck cloth	5½ yards	*Follow directions below or use pattern provided* for tepee front bottom (A). Cut 3 isosceles triangles (see page 139) with 44¾″ base and 45⅞″ height or use patterns provided for tepee sides (B), 4 ties (D), 1 isosceles triangle with 15½″ base and 15⅞″ height or use pattern provided for tepee front top (E), and 4 pole pockets (F).
Olive green felt	3 yards	Cut 3 side grass (C), 2 (1 and 1 reversed) front grass (X), 8 flags (H), and 4 flag pockets (G).
Red felt	9″ × 12″	Cut 2 ladybug bases (I).
Black felt	9″ × 12″	Cut 2 ladybug antennae (J), 1 ladybug head (K), 4 ladybug spots (L), 3 bee stripes (O), and 1 stinger (N).
Yellow felt	9″ × 12″	Cut 2 bee bases (M) and 1 butterfly body (W).
White felt	9″ × 12″	Cut 1 bee wing (P) and 2 (1 of each) dragonfly wings (R).
Aqua felt	9″ × 12″	Cut 2 dragonfly bases (Q).
Orange felt	9″ × 12″	Cut 1 beetle base (S), 1 beetle head (U), and 2 butterfly bases (V).
Kelly green felt	3″ × 3″	Cut 4 beetle legs (T).
Lime green felt	3″ × 3″	
White fabric	1¼ yards	Cut 1 square 40″ × 40″ and 4 rectangles 1″ × 4″ for loops (Z).
Main quilt fabric	1¼ yards	Cut 1 square 40″ × 40″.
1″ batting	1½ yards	Cut 1 square 40″ × 40″.
Hook-and-loop tape	5″	Cut 5 pieces, 1″ each.
½″-diameter PVC poles, 5′ long each	4	
Yarn to tie quilt		
Embroidery floss—green, red, black, blue, yellow, orange		

Tepee Front Bottom Template

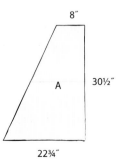

Follow the instructions to draw a template or use pattern provided on the CD to make the tepee front bottom pieces (A). To cut the tepee front bottoms (A), draw a base line 22¾″ long. From an end of the base line, draw a perpendicular line straight up 30½″. Draw an 8″ line from the perpendicular, parallel to the base line. Join the endpoints of the 8″ line and the base line. Repeat the process to create a mirror image of the tepee front bottom (A).

Tent Assembly

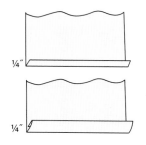

1. Finish the side edges of the tepee front bottoms (A) and the bottom edges of the tepee front bottoms (A) and tepee sides (B). To do so, fold the edge toward the wrong side ¼" and press. Fold the edge up another ¼" and topstitch along the fold.

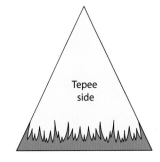

2. Pin a side grass (C) piece to the bottom edge of a side panel (B), as shown. Attach the grass with a topstitch, sewing up and down each blade of grass. Repeat with the other 2 side grass (C) pieces and 2 side (B) panels. Attach the front grass (X) pieces to the front bottom (A) panels in a similar fashion.

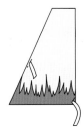

3. Finish the raw edges of the ties (D) with a blanket stitch. Sew a tie (D) onto the first placement mark as indicated on the pattern, on the right side of a front panel (A). Repeat, sewing a tie (D) onto the wrong side of the front panel (A) at the center front bottom placement mark, as indicated on the pattern. Repeat for the other front panel (A). The ties can be used to keep the front panels open once the project is complete.

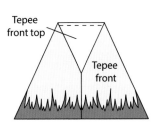

4. With the tepee front panels (A) facing up, make sure the bottom hems are in line and the center front edges meet. Pin the lower edge of the tepee front panel top (E) to the top edge of the aligned tepee front panels (A), right sides together. Machine sew the pieces together.

5. Cut 4⅛" off the top of each tepee side (B) and the front top (E).

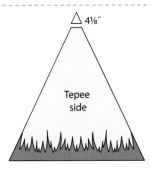

6. Following the directions in Step 1, finish the top edge of each of the 4 panels. Set aside.

7. Following the directions in Step 1, finish the short ends of each of the pole pockets (F).

8. Fold each pole pocket (F) in half lengthwise, wrong sides together, and sew a basting stitch by machine to secure the long edges together.

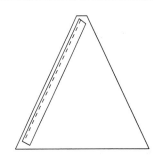

9. Place a pole pocket (F) on the wrong side of a tepee side panel (B). Align the top edges of the pole pocket (F) and the side panel (B). Align the long edges of the pole pocket (F) with the left-most long side of the tepee side panel (B). Machine sew the 3 long edges together. Repeat with the other 2 tepee side panels (B) and the tepee front panel (A).

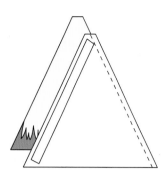

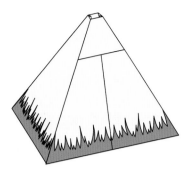

10. Sew 2 tepee sides together, right sides facing and long edges aligned.

11. Repeat Step 10 until all 4 panels are sewn together.

Tepee Flags

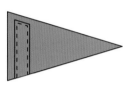

1. Edgestitch a flag pocket (G) to the wrong side of a flag (H). Repeat 3 times.

2. Place a flag piece (H) from Step 1 wrong sides together with a flag (H) without a pocket. Use a blanket stitch to sew around the perimeter of the flag, leaving the bottom open near the edge so the pole can slip into place.

3. Repeat Steps 1 and 2 to create the other 3 flags. Set aside.

Fun Bugs

note: *For this project you need only the hook part of the hook-and-loop tape. Cut the tape into 5 sections, 1″ each.*

1. Sew a 1″ piece of hook tape to the right side of a ladybug base (I) by machine.

2. With a needle and thread, attach the ladybug antennae (J) to the wrong side of the ladybug base (I) with attached hook tape.

3. Using a blanket stitch, attach the ladybug head (K) and ladybug spots (L) to the right side of the other ladybug base (I).

4. Place the ladybug bases (I) wrong sides together. Use a blanket stitch to sew around the perimeter of the bug to complete it.

5. Sew a 1″ piece of hook tape to the right side of a bee base (M).

6. Use a running stitch to attach the bee stinger (N) to the wrong side of the bee base (M) with attached hook tape.

7. Use a running stitch to attach the bee stripes (O) to the right side of the other bee base (M).

8. Use a split stitch to sew the wing detail onto the wing (P).

9. Attach the wing (P) to the bee base (M) with attached stripes (O), using a running stitch.

10. Place the 2 bee bases (M) wrong sides together. Use a blanket stitch to stitch around the perimeter of the bee. As you're making your way around, switch to a running stitch when you get to the stinger (N) and continue on with a blanket stitch to complete the bee.

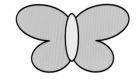

11. Cut a 1˝ section of hook tape so it measures ⅛˝ × 1˝. Sew the hook tape to the right side of the dragonfly base (Q) by machine. Set aside.

12. Using a split stitch, sew the details on the dragonfly wings (R).

13. Use a running stitch to attach the wings (R) to the right side of the other dragonfly base (Q).

14. Place the dragonfly bases (Q) wrong sides together. Use a blanket stitch to sew around the perimeter of the dragonfly base to complete the dragonfly.

15. Sew a 1˝ piece of hook tape to the right side of a beetle base (S) by machine.

16. Use a whipstitch to attach 4 beetle legs (T) to the wrong side of the base (S) with attached hook tape. Set aside.

17. Use a scalloped rotary blade to cut thin zigzag strips from the lime green felt. The strips should measure ⅛˝ and ¼˝ wide. Use a running stitch to attach the stripes to the right side of a beetle base (S) and a beetle head (U), as shown below.

18. Trim the excess of the stripes from the base (S) and head (U).

19. Use a running stitch to attach the beetle head (U) to the top of the beetle base (S) with attached stripes.

20. Place the beetle base (S) with attached head and stripes over the beetle base (S) with attached legs (T), wrong sides together.

21. Use a blanket stitch to sew the perimeter of the beetle to complete it.

22. Sew a 1˝ piece of hook tape to the right side of a butterfly base (V). Set aside.

23. Use a blanket stitch to attach the butterfly body (W) to the right side of the other butterfly base (V).

24. Place the butterfly base (V) with attached body (W) over the butterfly base (V) with attached hook tape, wrong sides together.

25. Use a blanket stitch to sew around the perimeter of the butterfly to complete it.

Comfy Quilt

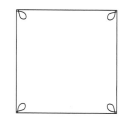

1. To create the loops (Z) for the quilt, fold a loop (Z) in half lengthwise, right sides together. Sew the long edges together by machine. Turn right side out and press well. Repeat for the other 3 loops (Z).

2. To fold the loop (Z), overlap the ends so that the same side remains up. Create a loop rather than just fold the strip in half.

3. Pin a loop to the right side in each corner of the white square, matching the raw edges. Baste into place by machine.

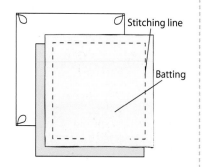

Stitching line

Batting

4. To assemble the quilt, place the white fabric square and the main quilt fabric square right sides together. Lay the batting on top of the wrong side of the main quilt fabric.

5. Sew around the perimeter, by machine, with a ½″ seam allowance. Leave an opening at the bottom to turn the quilt right side out.

6. Clip the corners and turn the quilt right side out. Use scissors to turn out the corners, being careful to not poke through them.

7. Use a blind stitch to sew the opening closed.

8. Measure 10″ from the top edge and 10″ from the left edge, and make a small mark where the 2 measurements meet. Repeat to make 3 rows of 3 marks, each 10″ apart. Using a yarn needle and yarn, make knots through all the quilt layers at each mark to complete the quilt.

Put It All Together

Slide the PVC poles through the tepee pockets and set them in the loops of the quilt below. Add the insects to the felt grass. Place the flags over the top ends of the poles to complete the tepee.

Photo by Jessica Peck

Glamping

Do you have a princess who likes to camp on her own terms? Or perhaps it is you I am speaking of …. I love all of the romance associated with camping, but I could leave the outdoors *out*. I created this tent for my little girl to have a chic place to camp indoors. The structure is composed of PVC pipe so it is easy to put up and take down, perfect to bring out on a rainy day! The sheer fabric is just right for gazing at stars, even if they may be artificial.

MATERIALS • Makes one tent and one play quilt.

Material	Amount	Cut
Sheer fabric for tent, 58″ wide	5 yards	Cut into 2 rectangles 58″ × 82½″.
White fabric for quilt, 42″ wide	2½ yards	Cut into 2 squares 41″ × 41″.
High-loft quilt batting	41″ × 41″ square	
¾″-diameter PVC pipes, 36″ long	4	
¾″-diameter PVC pipes, 48″ long	2	
½″-diameter PVC pipe, 48″ long	1	
¾″-diameter 90° S × S PVC elbows	4	
¾″ × ¾″ × ½″ side-outlet 90° elbow S × S × F PVC fittings	2	
½″-diameter male PVC adapters (with male side threaded)	2	
Embroidery floss—red, orange, yellow, green, blue, pink, purple, fuchsia, teal	1 skein of each	

Use schedule 40 PVC pipe. The PVC pipes and connections are easy to find at your local hardware store.

Glamping Tent Assembly

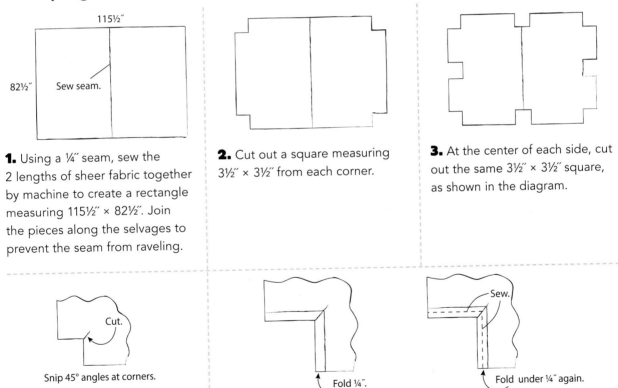

1. Using a ¼″ seam, sew the 2 lengths of sheer fabric together by machine to create a rectangle measuring 115½″ × 82½″. Join the pieces along the selvages to prevent the seam from raveling.

2. Cut out a square measuring 3½″ × 3½″ from each corner.

3. At the center of each side, cut out the same 3½″ × 3½″ square, as shown in the diagram.

4. Make a ½″ cut at a 45° angle in the interior corners of all the cutouts you made. This will allow for a seam to be finished nicely in the cutouts.

5. Starting in a cut-out interior corner from Steps 3 and 4, fold the raw edge in ¼″ to the wrong side and press. Fold the edge under another ¼″ and press well. Pin the seam and repeat on the other perpendicular raw edge of the corner cutout. Sew the folded seams by machine to finish them.

6. Repeat Step 5 for all of the cutouts. Stitch across the corners to reinforce them so they won't ravel.

7. Fold the raw edges on the fabric perimeter ¼″ toward the wrong side. Press. Turn each folded edge under 2″ toward the wrong side to make a casing for the PVC pipes. Press well and pin into place.

8. Sew each casing seam close to the ¼″ fold to complete the fabric for the tent.

9. To assemble the tent, start at an end and work your way up and over. Place a 48″ pipe in the casing pocket of a long edge of the fabric.

10. Cinch the fabric to fit on the pipe and add a 90° elbow on each end, with the elbow pointing up at a 45° angle.

11. Next, add a 36″ pipe in each end of the elbow, through the casing pockets in the short sides of the fabric. These pipes create the tent openings.

12. Place a ¾″ × ¾″ × ½″ side-outlet 90° elbow at the top junction of the ¾″-diameter, 36″-long pipes. Add the side-outlet elbows so the ½″ elbow points toward the inside of the tent.

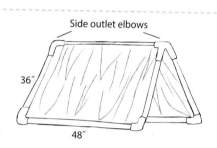

Side outlet elbows

36″

48″

13. Insert each end of the 48″ pipe, ½″ in diameter, into a ½″ male PVC adapter. Place each adapter end into the ½″ elbow of a ¾″ × ¾″ × ½″ side-outlet 90° elbow. (*Note:* This rod will not go through a pocket.)

14. Continue working your way back down the other side of the fabric in the same manner to complete the tent. Adjust the sheer fabric as necessary to have the gathers appear even.

 If the fabric and casing for the 36″ pipes is tight, try cutting the pipes shorter by ½″ or 1″ to allow more "wiggle room."

Be sure to smooth the cut edges of the pipe with sandpaper to prevent snagging the fabric as the pipes push through the casings.

Glamping Quilt Assembly

1. Follow Steps 43–46 of Tepee Assembly (page 118) to create the base quilt. Measure a grid of approximately 10˝ × 10˝ squares to create intersections for the pom-poms. Gently mark the center of each intersection with a marking pen.

2. To create the pom-poms, wrap embroidery floss around 4 of your fingers 40 times.

3. Tuck the tail between two of your fingers while keeping the floss wrapped around the others.

Cut.

4. Cut a long piece of thread and wrap it a few times around the center of the thread wrapped around your fingers. Slide the loops off your fingers and then tie a knot in the center thread. Trim the thread tails close to the center thread knot.

5. Cut the loops at either end of the bundle.

6. Roll the pom-pom in your hands to separate the strands of threads in the pom-pom to give it a softer feel, making it poofier.

7. Repeat Steps 2–6 with floss in various colors to make the rest of the pom-poms.

8. With a needle and embroidery floss, sew through all layers of the quilt, making a knot around the pom-pom to secure it to the top of the quilt. Repeat for the rest of the pom-poms.

9. Place the quilt under the tent, and lie back and watch the stars!

A Home of Her Own

We are all aware that reading is an integral part of a child's development. Even when my children were very small, I encouraged them to play with books, take them down off the shelf, tear the pages, love them. I believe if books are kept on the shelf to stay "nice," children aren't allowed to develop such a special relationship with them. I feel it is because of this relationship that both of my children developed a love for reading at an early age. I wanted to create a special nook for my daughter to store her books, someplace where she could crawl inside and be transported away to the world in her book.

MATERIALS • Makes one hanging canopy and one floor cushion.

Patterns can be found on pages CD205–CD265.

Material	Amount	Cut
Canopy and cushion fabric, 42″–44″ wide	10½ yards	Cut 2 loops (A), 2 top fronts (B), 1 pipe sleeve (C), 4 (2 and 2 reversed) top ends (D), 3 rectangles 81″ × 42″ (2¼ yards × width of fabric) for curtain panels, 2 cushion tops (L), and 4 cushion sides (M).
Contrasting fabric for scallop, 54″ wide	1 yard	Cut 2 scallops (F).
Lining fabric, 54″ wide	2 yards	Cut 2 scallops (F) and 2 bias strips (K).
6 colors of felt for houses, 36″ wide	½ yard each	Cut 1 house (G), 1 house (H), 4 houses (I), and 4 houses (J).
Piping	3 yards	
5″-thick foam	24″ circle	
½″-diameter PVC pipe	18″ piece	
Hula-Hoop, 28″ diameter	1	
Hooks	2 S hooks and 2 screw hooks	
Duct tape		

* Use purchased piping or use your favorite technique to make your own. I used ⅜″ cording inside the piping.

Canopy Assembly
Canopy Top

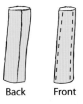

Back   Front

1. Fold a loop (A) in half lengthwise, right sides together. Sew the long open edge closed. Turn right side out.

2. Press the loop with the seam in the middle back. Topstitch along each long side.

3. Fold the loop in half with center seams facing, and baste the raw edges together.

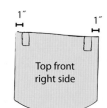

4. Repeat Steps 1–3 to make another loop (A).

5. Place the loops 1″ from each end of a top front (B), right sides together and raw edges aligned. Baste the loops in place.

6. Fold under a short end of the pipe sleeve (C) ¼″ to the wrong side and press. Fold the edge under again ¼″ and press. Topstitch in place. Repeat for the other short end.

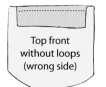

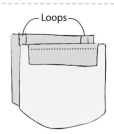

7. Fold the pipe sleeve in half lengthwise, wrong sides together.

8. Center and pin the pipe sleeve to the *wrong* side of the top front (B) without loops, aligning the raw edges along the top edge. Sew the pipe sleeve to the top front along the top edge.

9. Pair up the top front with loops and the top front with attached pipe sleeve (C), right sides together. The loops will be between the 2 layers and the pipe sleeve will be on top. Sew the top seam. Press open.

10. Place a canopy top end (D) and a reversed canopy top end (D) right sides together. Sew the canopy ends together along the edge labeled side A. Press open. Repeat with the remaining 2 top ends (D).

11. Place a stitched pair of canopy top ends (D) right sides together with the assembled top front sections (B), aligning the seams along the straight edges. Sew the raw edges together. Press open.

12. Repeat to attach the other pair of canopy top ends to the other side of the top front. Set aside.

Canopy Scallop

1. Sew the 2 scallops (F) together end to end. Repeat with scallop (F) lining pieces.

2. Fold the joined scallop in half with right sides together so the short ends meet. Sew the short ends together, forming a ring. Repeat with the scallop (F) lining.

3. Place the scallop lining and scallop right sides together. Sew along the bottom curved edge of the scallop to join the layers, pivoting at each point.

4. Clip the curves of the scallops and turn right side out. Press well. Set aside.

Canopy Curtain

1. Place 2 of the curtain panels (E) wrong sides together. Sew down the long edge with a ¼˝ seam allowance. Press the seam to the side.

2. Unfold the 2 panels and refold them, right sides together, back over the seam. Sew down the folded edge with a ½˝ seam allowance, creating a French seam. Press the seam to the side. Sew the seam flat against the panel by topstitching along the edge.

3. Repeat Steps 1–2 to attach the third panel (E).

4. To finish the last long raw edges, fold under a long edge ¼˝ toward the wrong side and press. Fold the edge under again ¼˝ and press. Topstitch in place. Repeat with the other long raw edge and the bottom edge of the curtain.

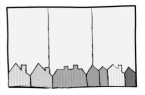

5. Cut out the houses from the felt. Cut out each window and door, or for more variety, select only certain windows and doors to remove or just cut out some windows—it's up to you! Place the houses on the perimeter of the canopy curtain. Start by carefully aligning a house along the bottom hemmed corner of the curtain. Continue to place the houses to your liking. Trim the house sides if necessary to fit the canopy curtain hem.

6. Topstitch around the perimeter of the first house. After you have sewn around the house, topstitch around the windows and door. Take care to trim all threads.

7. Attach each house in turn, making your way around the bottom perimeter of the canopy curtain.

Assemble the Canopy

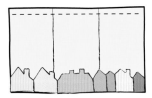

1. Sew a gathering stitch by machine along the top raw edge of the canopy curtain. Adjust the gathers and pin the canopy curtain to the top edge of the scallop (F), with right sides facing out.

2. Baste the top edge of the canopy curtain to the scallop. Set aside.

3. Stitch the bias strips (K) together end to end. Fold under a short end ¼˝ to the wrong side. Press. Fold the end under again ¼˝ and press. Topstitch in place. Repeat with the other short end.

4. Fold the bias strip (K) in half, lengthwise, matching the raw edges. Press.

5. Pin the bias strip to the inside top edge of the canopy curtain, matching the hemmed edges of the bias strip with the open ends of the curtain.

6. Sew around the perimeter of the scallop edge to attach the bias strip to the curtain and scallop.

7. Turn the canopy curtain wrong side out. Place the canopy top inside the canopy curtain with right sides together, taking care to center a top front (B) piece over the curtain opening and to align raw edges. Sew the canopy curtain and canopy top sections together. Turn right side out.

8. Use a saw or hand-held pipe cutter to make a cut through the Hula-Hoop ring. Insert a cut end of the hoop into the bias strip (K), feeding the fabric over the hoop to cover it. After the hula hoop is inserted, tape the ends together with duct tape for stability. Turn the canopy right side out. Insert the 18˝ PVC pipe into the pipe sleeve in the canopy top. Insert the S hooks into the loops and hang the canopy from the screw hooks.

Cushion Assembly

1. Sew the 4 cushion sides (M) together end to end.

2. Fold the cushion side in half with right sides together so the short ends meet. Sew the short edges together to form a circle. Turn right side out.

3. Beginning at a seam, sew a gathering stitch along the top edge of the cushion side. Repeat along the bottom edge.

4. Holding the top thread, carefully pull and gather the cushion side. Alternate between gathering the top and bottom side until it is all gathered. Adjust the gathers to fit around the cushion top (L).

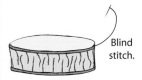

5. Pin the piping to the right side of the cushion side along both the top and bottom edges. Baste in place.

6. Turn the cushion side wrong side out. Sew the cushion top (L) to the top edge, right sides together.

7. Stitch the other cushion top (L) to the lower edge of the cushion side, sewing only halfway around.

Blind stitch.

8. Turn the cushion right side out. Insert the foam and blindstitch the opening closed to complete it.

Play Stand

My children often set up imaginary worlds under tables with blankets or other furniture and household objects. For this project, I really wanted to create a structure to support the felt playsets. After creating the basic structure, the details can be swapped out to become a game stand, farmer's market, or ice cream shoppe.

MATERIALS • Makes one stand.

Material	Amount	Cut
White fabric	6 yards	Cut 2 rectangles 8½″ × 37″ (C), 4 rectangles 8½″ × 19″ (E), 2 rectangles 30½″ × 37″ (A), 4 rectangles 19″ × 30½″ (D), and 12 rectangles 4½″ × 19″ (B) (no patterns provided).
Fusible fleece interfacing	3 yards	Follow instructions below.
1″ buttons	15	
½″ PVC poles, 53″ long	4	
¾″ PVC poles, 36″ long	2	
¾″ PVC poles, 18″ long	4	
¾″ × ½″ PVC 90° elbows	4	
¾″ × ¾″ × ½″ PVC connectors	4	

Frame Assembly

1. Sew a large rectangle (A) to 2 smaller rectangles (B) as shown, with right sides together. Press seams toward side panels.

2. Sew the top rectangle (C) to the top of the smaller rectangles (B), with right sides together. Press seams toward side panels.

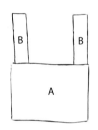

3. Fuse the fusible fleece to the wrong side of this section. To do so, lay the fleece with its fusible side up. Lay the fabric panel right side up on the fleece. Trim the fleece to fit the panel. Iron to fuse the fabric and fleece, following the manufacturer's directions.

4. Repeat Steps 1 and 2 to create a lining for the front of the structure.

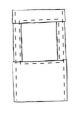

5. Place both bases right sides together. Sew around the inner window. Leaving an 8˝ opening at the bottom edge for turning.

6. Turn the base right side out by pulling the side without the interfacing through the opening. Be sure to trim the seam allowance and clip the corners to give the fabric ease. Press well. Fold under the raw edges of the opening and topstitch around the window opening.

7. Fold each of the long edges to the inside ¼˝ and press. Fold in another ¼˝ and press again. Pin the layers together and edgestitch each side.

8. Baste through all layers at the top and bottom of the panel.

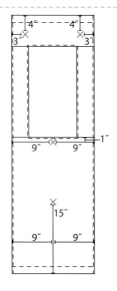

9. Fold both layers under ¼˝ at the top edge and press.

10. Fold the top under another 1½˝ and press. Topstitch the hem, creating a pocket for the PVC pole. Repeat Steps 9 and 10 to create a pocket at the bottom of the panel.

11. Create the two side panels following Steps 1–10. Use rectangles (D), (E), and (B), as shown.

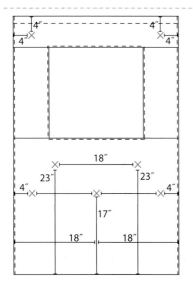

12. Sew buttons to the panels following the diagram.

13. Assemble the structure, using the ¾˝ poles horizontally and the ½˝ poles vertically. Slide the ¾˝ poles through the pockets at the top and bottom of each panel before you attach the corner connectors and elbows.

Game Stand Details

MATERIALS

Patterns can be found on pages CD266, CD267, CD280, and CD281. This project uses the pattern for the Farmer's Market curtains.

Material	Amount	Cut
White fabric	¼ yard	Cut 2 chalkboards (A) lining.
Striped fabric	½ yard	Cut 8 banners (B) and 4 curtains (Q).
Contrasting bunting fabric	¼ yard	Cut 8 banners (B).
Chalkboard fabric	½ yard	Cut 2 chalkboards (A).
Double-fold bias tape	1½ yards	
Grosgrain ribbon, ½″ wide	1 yard	Cut 2 pieces, 18″ each.

Game Stand Details Assembly

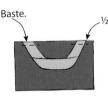

Baste. ½″

1. Measure ½″ in from each end of the fabric chalkboard (A) on the right side. Baste each end of the ribbon by machine, being careful not to twist the ribbon.

2. Place a chalkboard lining (A) over a fabric chalkboard (A), right sides together, with the ribbon sandwiched between the two layers. Sew around the perimeter of the chalkboard, being careful not to catch the ribbon. Leave an opening at the bottom to turn the chalkboard right side out.

3. Turn right side out. Fold the seam allowance in and blindstitch the opening closed. Repeat Steps 1–3 to make another chalkboard.

4. Place 2 banners (B) right sides together. Sew the 2 angled edges by machine, and turn right side out. Press well. Repeat to make 7 more banners (B), alternating between the main and contrasting fabrics.

5. Open the bias tape and insert the tops of the banners (B) into the fold of the bias tape. Pin in place, alternating between the main and contrasting fabrics.

6. Fold the short ends of the bias tape in ¼″ and press. Repeat, folding over another ¼″, and press.

7. Fold the bias tape back in half, encasing the pennants, and pin.

8. Sew the bias tape by machine, connecting the banners (B).

9. Follow Steps 20–23 in Farmer's Market Details (page 135) to make curtains (Q).

10. Hang the banner, chalkboard, and curtains up on the buttons to complete the game stand details.

Farmer's Market Details

MATERIALS

Patterns can be found on pages CD268–CD284.

Material	Amount	Cut
White felt	9″ × 12″	Cut 1 market scale face (J).
Gray felt	2 sheets 9″ × 12″	Cut 1 market scale (I) and 1 basket ring (E).
Kelly green felt	9″ × 12″	Cut 1 leaf (H) and 1 each of lettuce (P1), (P2), and (P3).
Purple felt	9″ × 12″	Cut 11 circles for grapes (L).
Tan felt	1½ yards	Cut 1 each of basket panels (D), 1 each of crate slats (N), and 1 each of small crate slats (O).
Brown felt	½ yard	Cut 4 table legs (A), 2 table tops (B), 1 market basket base (C), 1 grape stem (L), 1 apple stem (G), 1 crate logo (R) and 1 crate base (M).
Red felt	¼ yard	Cut 10 apples (F) and 1 scale dial (K).
Cord for bunting	1½ yards	
Curtain fabric	½ yard	Cut 4 curtains (Q).
Bunting fabric	½ yard	Cut 15 rectangles approximately 1½″ × 10″ (no pattern provided).
Contrasting fabric for bunting	½ yard	Cut 15 rectangles approximately 1½″ × 10″ (no pattern provided).

Farmer's Market Details Assembly

1. Place 2 table legs (A) wrong sides together. Topstitch around the perimeter. Repeat with the other table legs (A).

2. Place 2 table tops (B) wrong sides together. Topstitch around the perimeter.

3. Place the table legs (A) underneath the table top (B) where indicated on the table top pattern, so they overlap by ½″. Sew the legs (A) to the top (B) following the topstitching on the table top (B).

4. Cut the slits in the table top (B) as indicated on the pattern to complete the table. Button it to the structure.

5. Lay the basket base (C) right side up. Place the basket panels (D) over the base (C), right side up. Pin. Topstitch around the perimeter of each panel.

6. Place the basket ring (E) over the basket panels (D), about 1″ from the top edge of the basket. Topstitch around the perimeter.

7. Add 6 apples (F), 2 leaves (H), and the apple stem (G) to the basket, and arrange as shown. Topstitch the pieces together where they overlap.

8. Cut the slit as indicated on the basket pattern to complete the basket. Button it to the structure and slip the basket behind the table top (B).

9. Topstitch the market scale dial (K) to the scale face (J). Topstitch the scale face (J) to the scale (I).

10. Make the grapes (L) by overlapping and top-stitching the felt circles as shown on the pattern. Place the grapes (L) behind the scale (I), overlapping by ½˝. Stitch in place.

11. Cut a slit in the grapes as indicated. Button the grapes with attached scale to the structure.

12. Lay the crate base (M) right side up. Place the crate slats (N) on the lower portion of the base (M), right sides up. Pin. Topstitch around the perimeter of each slat (N) by machine. Add the letters of the crate logo (R) that spell *Apples* and topstitch into place.

13. Lay the small crate slats (O) on the upper portion of the crate base (M) and pin into place. Topstitch around each slat (O).

14. Place the lettuce (P) behind the top edge of the crate base, overlapping by ½˝. Hold the lettuce in place with topstitching.

15. Place the remaining 4 apples (F) in the crate, trimming and arranging as shown (below). Topstitch the apples in place.

16. Cut slits as indicated on the small crate slat pattern (O). Button the crate into place on the structure.

17. Pair a bunting rectangle with a contrasting bunting rectangle, wrong sides together. Tie the rectangles onto the bunting cord.

18. Repeat to tie the remaining pairs of bunting rectangles to the bunting cord.

19. Wind ends of cord around the buttons above the large window to hang bunting.

20. Place 2 curtains (Q) right sides together. Sew around the perimeter, leaving an opening for turning.

21. Turn right side out. Press. Blindstitch the opening closed.

22. Repeat Steps 20 and 21 to create another curtain (Q).

23. Following the sewing machine manufacturer's directions, create 2 buttonholes as indicted on the pattern. Repeat for the other curtain (Q).

24. Button the curtains in place above each small window to complete the farmer's market details.

Ice Cream Shoppe Details

MATERIALS

Patterns can be found on pages CD280–CD289. This project uses the patterns for the Farmer's Market table and curtains.

Material	Amount	Cut
White felt	9″ × 12″	Cut 1 whipped cream (I). Use remaining felt for the jar backgrounds (see Step 3).
Tan felt	9″ × 12″	Cut 1 sauce (G) and 1 dollop (R).
Brown felt	9″ × 12″	Cut 1 sauce (G) and 1 scoop (O).
Dark pink felt	9″ × 12″	Cut 4 flowers (N) and 3 window basket details (M).
Purple felt	9″ × 12″	Cut 3 flowers (N).
Turquoise felt	9″ × 12″	Cut 2 flowers (N).
Yellow felt	9″ × 12″	Cut 4 flowers (N) and 1 dollop (R).
Red felt	9″ × 12″	Cut 1 sauce (G), 1 dollop (R), 1 cherry (H), and 3 flowers (N).
Gray felt	9″ × 12″	Cut 3 jar lids (J) and 1 spoon (K).
Ivory felt	9″ × 12″	Cut 1 banana (E) and 1 scoop (O).
Pink felt	1 yard	Cut 4 table legs (A), 2 table tops (B), 1 scoop (O), and 2 window baskets (L).
Aqua felt	9″ × 12″	Cut 1 bowl (D).
Assorted-color buttons	16	
Heavyweight vinyl, such as Quilter's Vinyl	¼ yard	Cut 3 jars (F).
3 fabrics for bunting	¼ yard each	Cut 10 scallops (P) from various fabrics.
Double-fold bias tape	1½ yards	
Curtain fabric	½ yard	Cut 4 curtains (Q).

Ice Cream Shoppe Details Assembly

1. Follow Steps 1–4 of Farmer's Market Details Assembly (page 134) to assemble and attach the table top (B) and table legs (A).

2. To assemble the ice cream sundae, place the banana (E) behind the upper edge of the bowl (D). Layer the 3 scoops (O) with their dollops (R) and pin them into place. Place the whipped cream (I) over the top scoop and add the cherry (H). Topstitch all pieces in place to complete the sundae. Cut a ¾″ slit in the top center scoop and button it into place.

3. To assemble each jar of sauce, begin with the vinyl jar (F) and add the lid (J). Sew the sauce (G) behind the jar (F). Repeat with all jars (F), lids (J), and sauces (G). Arrange the 3 jars as shown (see photo above) onto a sheet of white felt and topstitch in place. Place the spoon (K) behind the lid of a jar. Trim away excess white felt. Cut a ¾″ slit in the top center jar pattern and button into place.

4. To assemble the window basket, place the 2 window baskets (L) wrong sides together and topstitch around the perimeter. Place the 3 basket details (M) in place and topstitch around the perimeter of each.

5. Sew a button to the center of each flower (N).

6. Layer the flowers (N) and stitch the overlaps.

7. Place the bundle of flowers along the top edge of the window basket (L) and stitch along the bottom edge of the flowers. Cut a ¾″ slit near the top center of the flowers and button into place.

8. Place 2 curtains (Q) right sides together. Sew around the perimeter, leaving an opening to turn right side out.

9. Turn the curtains right side out and press well. Blindstitch the opening closed. Make the button-holes where indicated on the pattern.

10. Repeat Steps 7–9 with remaining curtain (Q) pieces and button into place above each small window.

11. Place 2 scallops (P) right sides together. Sew around the curve by machine.

12. Clip the curve and turn right side out. Press well.

13. Repeat Steps 11 and 12 to create the rest of the scallops (E).

14. Open the bias tape and place the scallops in the fold.

15. Refold the bias tape, enclosing the straight edge of each of the 5 scallops. Topstitch along the bias tape to secure.

16. Trim the ends of the bias tape and wrap around the buttons above the large window to complete the ice cream shoppe details.

Special Techniques

Drafting Circles

For a quick way to draft circles, fold the fabric in half, and then in half again perpendicular to the first fold. For this technique, you will want to use half of the diameter, or the radius measurement. Mark the circle radius in a curve from fold to fold. Cut on the drawn curve and unfold the piece. Or you could simply fold the fabric in half one time and draw a semicircle on the fold using the width of the circle diameter.

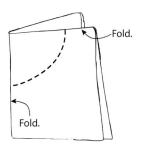

Fold.

Fold.

Drafting Isosceles Triangles

1. To draft a triangle, first measure the length of the base.

2. From the center of the base, measure the height. Be sure to use a ruler with a grid so you have a nice right angle to measure up from.

3. After marking the height of the triangle, draw a diagonal line to each end of the base to complete the triangle.

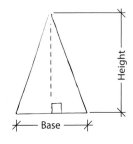

Height

Base

Freezer-Paper Stenciling

MATERIALS
- Freezer paper
- Small utility knife
- Fabric paint
- Iron

Freezer-paper stenciling is such a versatile technique! It is a great way to add detail to any project, making it a bit more personal.

1. Cut the design from the freezer paper.

2. Place the freezer paper shiny side down on the fabric, and press.

3. Paint on the fabric. Depending on the fabric and color, you may need more than one coat.

4. After the final coat is dry, carefully peel away the freezer paper to reveal the design.

Embroidery Stitches

Blanket Stitch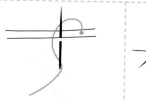

1. To join 2 pieces of felt at an edge seam, place them wrong sides together and begin by knotting the thread. Take the needle between the 2 felt layers and pull it through the bottom layer of the felt. The knot will be concealed between the 2 layers of felt.

2. Bring the needle and thread around to the top of the felt layers, push the needle through both layers to the bottom, and pull the thread through, leaving a small loop not pulled through.

3. Weave the needle through the small loop.

4. Pull the thread taut.

5. To the right of the first stitch, push the needle through both felt layers from top to bottom, leaving a small loop out.

6. Weave the needle through the loop. Repeat this stitch to complete the seam(s), and knot the thread at the end to secure it.

 tip When creating my blanket stitches, I prefer to pull the thread a little more taught. Little ones are not the most gentle with their toys; they give them lots of love! If you create stitches a bit tighter than you normally would, the toy will hold up a bit better!

Some felt play pieces, such as the cake slice, have foam inside them, and in some cases the felt is pinned to this foam during construction. For these pieces, depending on the size of your stitches, you may wish to sew through the felt, the foam, and the other side of the felt to create the stitch.

Split Stitch

1. Knot the thread end. Beginning at the back of the felt, pull the thread through to the front until the knot catches.

2. Make the stitch about ⅛″ away by pushing the needle through the front of the felt and pulling it all the way through to the back side.

3. When you bring the needle through to the front again, make sure to bring it up through the middle of the first stitch, splitting it.

4. Continue the stitch by going down through the front to the back side of the felt and then up to the front through the middle of each previous stitch.

French Knot

1. Knot the thread end. Beginning at the back of the felt, pull the thread through to the front until the knot catches.

2. With your other hand, wrap the slack of the thread around the needle twice while keeping the thread taut.

3. Hold the tip of the needle near the point where the thread is coming through the front side of the felt.

4. Push the needle through the front of the fabric while keeping the slack of thread tight as you pull it through to the back, leaving a knot. Repeat for as many knots as you need.

Running Stitch

1. Knot the thread end. Beginning at the back of the felt, pull the thread through to the front until the knot catches.

2. Make the stitch about ⅛″ away by pushing the needle through the front of the felt and pulling it all the way through to the back side.

3. When you bring the needle to the front again, make sure to bring it up about ⅛″ away from the end of the first stitch.

4. Repeat this process until you have finished the stitch across the length of the felt.

Blind Stitch

This stitch is usually used to sew a seam from the front while hiding the stitches.

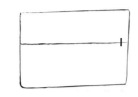

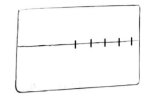

1. Knot the thread end. Beginning on one side of the seam, pull the thread through from the back side to the front, close to the seamline, until the knot catches.

2. Make a small stitch directly across from where the thread just exited, on the other side of the seam, and push the needle to the back side. Then push the needle through to the front, a small distance ahead of the last stitch.

3. Continue working your way back and forth between the sides of the seam, making small stitches. The key to these stitches is to make them directly in the fold of the seam allowance so they are rendered nearly invisible.

Whipstitch

1. Place the wrong sides of the felt layers together. Knot the thread end. Beginning on the back side of the felt, push the needle through to the front to catch the knot.

2. Take a small stitch over to the other side of the seam, ahead of where the thread exited, and push the needle through at an angle to the back side. Pull through both layers.

3. Take the needle back down through both felt layers at an angle.

4. Repeat for as many stitches as you need.

About the Author

Jessica Peck lives in Wisconsin with her favorite three redheads: her husband and two young children. All of her designs are created on the playroom floor. From conception to completion of each project, her children inspire her creativity.

Before launching her first line of sewing patterns, Sweetie Pie Bakery, Jessica graduated from Harrington College of Design in Chicago with a degree in interior design. You can see her eye for color and structure, as well as an expertise for construction, throughout her designs. Her passions for architecture and sewing were a natural combination for pattern design.

When Jessica is not sewing, she enjoys baking, photography, and relaxing with her family. Jessica Peck blogs daily at **jessicapeck.blogspot.com**.

stashBOOKS

fabric arts for a handmade lifestyle

If you're craving beautiful authenticity in a time of mass-production...Stash Books is for you. Stash Books is a line of how-to books celebrating fabric arts for a handmade lifestyle. Backed by C&T Publishing's solid reputation for quality, Stash Books will inspire you with contemporary designs, clear and simple instructions, and engaging photography.

www.stashbooks.com